COME PRAY

A GUIDE TO DEEPER PERSONAL
AND CORPORATE PRAYER

by Mary Glenn Hadley

Richmond, Indiana • www.fum.org

Copyright © 2001 Mary Glenn Hadley

Published 2001 by Friends United Press
Second Printing 2007

Cover design by Shari Pickett Veach
Book design by Susanna Combs

All rights reserved. No portion of this book may be reproduced, stored in electronic retrieval system or transmitted in any form or by means—electronic, mechanical, photocopy, recording or other—except for brief quotations in printed reviews, without the prior permission of the publisher.

Friends United Press
101 Quaker Hill Drive
Richmond IN 47374
friendspress@fum.org
www.fum.org

Library of Congress Cataloging-in-Publication Data

Hadley, Mary Glenn, 1939–
   Come pray / by Mary Glenn Hadley.
     p. cm.
   Includes bibliographical references.
   ISBN 0-944350-49-6
   ISBN 978-0-944350-49-2
     1. Prayer—Christianity. I. Title.

BV210.3.H33 2001
248.3'2—dc21   2001023783

*This book is dedicated
to my sisters and brother who have
faithfully supported me through all my ventures:
Edna Smith, Hazel Hadley,
Clara Lee Locker, and Merlin Hadley.*

TABLE OF CONTENTS

Preface		ix
Chapter 1	What Is Prayer and Why Pray?	1
Chapter 2	How Do I Get Started?	9
Chapter 3	Maturing in Prayer	20
Chapter 4	A Biblical Prayer Teaches Interactive Skills	30
Chapter 5	Praying with the Lord's Prayer	38
Chapter 6	Praying for Others	48
Chapter 7	Prayer and Fasting	56
Chapter 8	Praying When God Seems Distant	65
Chapter 9	My House Shall Be Called a House of Prayer	76
Chapter 10	Dimensions of a Praying Church	84
Chapter 11	Learning to Pray as a Group	97
Chapter 12	Power in Corporate Prayer	107
Chapter 13	Praying in the Community	116
Conclusion		125
Activity 1	Use Scripture to Inform Prayer	127
Activity 2	Pray with a Parable	130
Activity 3	Plan for a Corporate Prayer Event	138
Resources		151

PREFACE

Several years ago, I received an invitation to attend a conference in Chicago. I didn't know why I was invited, and I didn't really see much reason to attend. However, after throwing the invitation away, another appeared on my desk. Something within me kept reminding me of this opportunity. I began to sense the nudging of the Spirit to participate in this conference. Arriving there, I found myself a stranger among many people.

The first session introduced me to the Concerts of Prayer, led by David Bryant, founder and president of Concerts of Prayer International. With this format for praying, Scripture and worship music guided us as we gathered in small groups to pray. The two hours of praying in this manner left me no longer feeling a stranger. Not only had we lifted our hearts to God for revival and renewal in the church, but also I heard the hearts of others as they prayed and felt my heart resonate with theirs. A longing grew within me to develop a stronger prayer life for myself and to encourage prayer within the larger faith community.

Prayer evokes a growing relationship with God. Though many of us pray, we have to admit that there is more to prayer than we are experiencing. This book is written for those who long for a greater experience of prayer. You will be challenged to mature in your personal prayer lives and to move toward a greater prayer ministry as a body of Christ.

Beginning with the basic concepts of what prayer is and the purpose of prayer, this book will take you on a venture in your personal prayer life in the first eight chapters. You will be given some suggestions for getting started in praying. Expect your horizons to enlarge as you consider the maturing levels of prayer. Learn from Moses how to interact in your conversations with God. Find a fresh way to take the model prayer Jesus gave his disciples and use it as a pattern for your own prayers. Be open to learning about the power of intercession and fasting. Spend time examining what is happening when God seems far away when you pray.

In the past, faith communities met regularly for the purpose of praying together. These were powerful prayer experiences. Today, in many churches, to gather to pray corporately is met with discomfort. Chapters 9-13 focus on corporate prayer. Explore some possibilities for restoring the power of corporate praying within your church or meeting. Corporate prayer is the gathering of a significant part of a local church or group of churches with the intention to pray for a common purpose. Consider what a House of Prayer might look like as you explore the dimensions of a praying church. Praying conversationally can be one way to learn to pray as a group. Discover how prayer events can be held that will give opportunity for people to rediscover the power of corporate praying. Consider ways to extend corporate prayer beyond the gathered meetings within the church by praying within the community. Prayer Walking or Making Your House a House of Prayer are two possibilities for impacting your community and strengthening the power of corporate prayer.

Truly God invites you to come pray. God wants to participate in your daily lives just as God intervened in the lives of others whose stories are shared in this book. I have drawn from my own personal experiences with prayer that span my years on the mission field, events stateside, biblical prayers, and insights from many who have contributed to my growing prayer life. Begin this book by pausing to ask God to teach you new truths and to give you greater insights about prayer that will not only make your experience deeper but will extend into your church family.

A summary at the end of each chapter followed by Reflect and Response suggestions allow time to examine your prayer life and experiment with the new possibilities you discover as you read.

If even one thing speaks to you and starts you on a fresh venture with God in prayer, I will thank God and trust that God will become your intimate friend who will continue to reveal new truths and provide deeper insights that you can pass on to others.

April 2000

CHAPTER 1

What Is Prayer and Why Pray?

A new awareness of what prayer is came to me during a time when I was experiencing some medical problems. I had had surgery and had been diagnosed with cancer, for which I was sent to M.D. Anderson Cancer Center in Houston, Texas, to receive a second opinion for treatment. Much to my surprise, I was asked to join a study there, which meant that I would need to arrange to stay in Houston for five months of chemotherapy. There were a lot of decisions to be made in a hurry.

I was very aware that the office staff and many, many others were praying for me. The day came when the subclavian catheter was inserted, the pre-chemotherapy blood was drawn, and I was to visit the doctor. When I saw the doctor, he told me he was changing plans because the pathologists there were unable to identify the aggressive cells. God had intervened on my behalf. I sent an e-mail to the office to tell them what had developed and to inform them that I would be back to work the following Monday. I'm told that there was rejoicing among the staff as they acknowledged God's faithfulness.

During this time a volunteer had come to work in our office for a few weeks. The volunteer took in all this with caution. She admitted to me later that she was almost jealous of the staff, who seemed to pray with expectation that answers would come and who readily identified and praised God for responding. She prayed, but she prayed without expecting anything to happen other than the possibility that God would give her wisdom for whatever her concern was at the time. She wondered how other people experienced prayer and started inviting people to talk about prayer on the Internet.

The responses to her invitation left me spending sleepless nights. For the most part, those who responded didn't see that prayer made any difference in their lives. I realized how easy it is to make God too small, to limit God to what the human mind can comprehend and to fail to recognize God's omniscience, thereby missing the very gift that God has given for knowing God more intimately.

God has given us an intellect to use, but God wants to enhance that intellect by sharing the spiritual dimension. Paul speaks to that in I Corinthians 2:14: "The [person] without the Spirit does not accept the things that come from the Spirit of God, for they are foolishness to him, and he cannot understand them, because they are spiritually discerned."

Once while leading a seminar on prayer, I shared a story of how God had answered the prayers of those who were praying for their city in outstanding ways. When I finished, a man in the group spoke up and said that he didn't believe it. I felt compelled to ask him why. He said that he didn't think that such a phenomenon could happen. To many in our society it is difficult to accept that prayer makes a difference, that the laws of nature may sometimes be suspended. In their minds, miracles must be dismissed as absurd.

In some popular concepts about prayer, prayer simply means telling God what to do and expecting God to act accordingly. People think God has given them good minds and generous resources that enable them to figure out things on their own. They don't want to bother God for the little things of life. They would only think to pray when they need something big or when they face major crises. When difficult experiences or situations arise, there is a cry of the inner person to God. That cry from an honest heart is heard by a holy God. For many, it is at those moments that their journey in prayer begins. Prayer becomes telling God what they want and then expecting God to respond. That kind of prayer is a monologue and limits the opportunities God offers through prayer.

Built into the soul of every person is an awareness of God. Prayer, however, is a vital part of our walk with God. We cannot assume that everyone knows what prayer is and why we pray. Many times in small groups and worship services when the opportunity to pray together arises, few verbalize.

Consider for a moment your own attitude about prayer. Is prayer a monologue or a conversation between God and you? What immediately comes to your mind when you hear the word? Would words like "powerful," "loving," or "talking with God" describe your response, or would you say that it is a worthless exercise?

Pause for a moment and think back to your first experience with prayer. What comes to mind? Could it be a memory of your parents teaching you to give thanks to God before a meal? Or was it talking with God as your parents tucked you in bed at night?

The Bible is a textbook on prayer. In Jeremiah 33:3 we read: "Call to me and I will answer you and tell you great and unsearchable things you do not know." What a gift God gives individuals to enter into conversations with God and to expect a response that tells us great and unsearchable things that would not have been known otherwise.

Prayer goes beyond just a conversation. True prayer is communion, where there is pleasure just being in the company of the other. Prayer, then, is a relationship with God. It is not a manipulation. It is talking with God and fellowshipping in each other's company. There are several reasons why prayer is so important.[1]

God tells us to pray. There are many passages in both the Old Testament and the New Testament that invite prayer. Experience God's compassion as God seeks to communicate through the written word.

- Isaiah 55:6: "Seek the Lord while he may be found; call on him while he is near."
- Matthew 7:7: "Ask and it will be given to you; seek and you will find; knock and the door will be opened to you."
- John 16:24: "Until now you have not asked for anything in my name. Ask and you will receive, and your joy will be complete."
- 1 Thessalonians 5:17: "Pray continually."

- Philippians 4:6: "Do not be anxious about anything, but in everything, by prayer and petition, with thanksgiving, present your requests to God."

Can you feel God's love flowing through these words? They are not words intended to make us afraid to commune with God. They are given out of our Lord's deep love for us and God's longing to communicate with us. Remember how God came and walked nightly with Adam and Eve in the garden? God wanted their fellowship just as God invites ours. If we are authentic about wanting to be a disciple of Christ, we will want to be obedient to his invitation to communicate through prayer.

A second reason for praying is to get to know God intimately. The Spirit alerts us to the things in our lives that separate us from God. The initiative to pray really comes from God. Without the open door of prayer, we would not be able to confess our sins or talk over the things for which we seek guidance. As we get to know God well, we understand how God looks at the things we are involved with, and we begin to look at things through God's perspectives. This is an exciting venture, for God does not look at things as people often do.

Once we begin to understand God's perspectives, through prayer, we will move to God's agenda. It is easy to get so bogged down in our "wish lists" for God that we miss the whole point of prayer. When developing a relationship with God, we find our prayers will focus more and more on God and less and less on ourselves. Phillips Brooks said, "The purpose of prayer is not to get man's will done in heaven, but to get God's will done on earth."[2] Henry Blackaby describes the opportunity prayer gives us to understand God's will and then to adjust our lives to that truth in his book *Experiencing God*.[3] These adjustments begin when we believe that God is who he says he is and that God will do what he says. Aligning our lives to God's truth will follow. Scripture gives examples of this from Abram to David, Hannah to Mary, Peter, Andrew, James and John, and many others. As their relationship with God grew, their faith grew, and they were willing to make those changes in their lives required to align their lives with God's truth. Adjusting our lives to God's truths allows us to pray in accordance with God's will. 1 John 5:14 gives guidance for this. "This is the assurance we have in approaching God: that if we ask anything according to his will, he hears us."

Prayer keeps us alive spiritually, another reason to pray. There has to be growth in any relationship to keep it alive. The same is true in our relationship with God. Jesus described this need well when he said in John 15:5-7, "I am the vine; you are the branches. If a man remains in me and I in him, he will bear much fruit; apart from me you can do nothing. If anyone does not remain in me, he is like a branch that is thrown away and withers; such branches are picked up, thrown into the fire and burned. If you remain in me and my words remain in you, ask whatever you wish, and it will be given you." It is no burden to remain in Jesus. That is a joyous place to be, and through that vantage point, we learn more of him and keep alive spiritually.

Letting God know what our needs are provides another reason to pray. Too often this is thought to be the primary reason to pray. Every relationship has to have at least two parties. God wants to hear our hearts and we need to hear from God. The troubling part is that we may expect God to grant everything we ask, whereas God only promises to supply all our needs. When we are in close communion with God, we become aware that the things we thought we wanted really would not be the best for us. My experience is that God's way is always better than my wishes.

A sixth reason why people pray is because prayer frees God's power to work. God really wants to accomplish his purposes through people. Therefore, God needs to hear our asking for those things he wants to do. For example, we may long for someone to come into a personal relationship with Jesus. We cannot force that to happen, but we can tell God of our longing and that frees God to work in that person's life. 1 Timothy 2:3-4 says. "This is good, and pleases God our Savior, who wants all [people] to be saved and to come to a knowledge of the truth."

SUMMARY

Prayer is a relationship with God where we talk with God and fellowship in each other's presence. Six reasons why we pray are:

1. God invites us to pray because God loves us deeply.
2. Prayer opens the way for us to know God intimately. It is a way to know God's heart and to see the areas of our lives that offend God and find forgiveness so the relationship can continue to grow.
3. Prayer moves us to God's agenda. Prayer is designed more to adjust us to God than to adjust God to ourselves.
4. Prayer nurtures our inner being and keeps us alive spiritually.

5. Prayer is an opportunity to tell God our needs.
6. Prayer frees God's power to work.

REFLECT AND RESPOND

Reflect on your prayer life. Sit in a quiet place. Relax your hands in your lap with palms up, ready to receive God's love, grace, and insights. Absorb anew God's invitation to come into a more intimate relationship. Feel God's love for you and ask God to help you understand how to adjust your life to God's purposes. Let go of your need to direct God. Trust God to listen to your heart's desires. Accept that God may have a better way than yours. Share with another one thing that you received from God as you talked with God just now.

---

[1] Grace and Fred Holland, *Talking With God* (Kisumu, Kenya: Evangel Publishing House, 1972), p. 21-32.

[2] Paul Cedar, *A Life of Prayer* (Nashville, TN: Word Publishing, 1998), p. 13.

[3] Henry Blackaby, *Experiencing God* (Nashville, TN: Lifeway Press, 1990), pp. 126-144.

Other Resources

Judson Cornwall, *Praying the Scriptures*, used by permission of the publisher (Lake Mary, Florida: Creation House, 1988).

CHAPTER 2

How Do I Get Started?

*J*udson Cornwall, in his book *Praying the Scriptures*, tells about an experience he had when he was teaching about prayer in another community. He mentioned to the pastor how impressed he was with the fervency of prayer exhibited by one young couple in the service. The pastor's response seemed less enthusiastic. He said, "They are very earnest and disciplined in their praying but, quite frankly, it doesn't seem to accomplish much in their lives." Cornwall was surprised at this response. If a person was disciplined to pray consistently, there certainly should be results. Cornwall had the opportunity to meet with this couple. He discovered that they were extremely mystical, almost to the "spooky" level, and their earnest and often dramatic prayers lacked sequence or substance. That evening he went to his home and meditated about this couple and that experience. The next day, he asked the young man about his Bible-reading habits. The young man admitted that he didn't have time to read the Bible. He explained that he was a student at the university and his studies consumed his reading time. He said he gave himself to prayer and left it to others to read the Bible. Cornwall told him that was a dangerous imbalance. He earnestly urged him to divide his prayer time between devotionally reading the Bible and emotionally calling upon God. He said, "You need to know better the God to whom you are praying, and you need to hear the Lord speak to you through the Word. You are conducting a monologue and calling it prayer."

The young man was teachable. Cornwall later learned that the prayer life of this young couple did take on new meaning and power and their prayers were sensed throughout the entire church. [1]

We live in the fast lane. Our lives are filled with many activities. Television consumes a lot of our time. Our children are involved with sports, music, and other activities that require parents' attention. When does one find those quiet moments to be alone with God in prayer? In the whirlwind of our activities we often shortchange our relationship with God. We may breathe a quick prayer as we dash out the door in the mornings. We may talk with God as we fight traffic going to work. God hears those prayers, but if we want our prayer life to grow, we need to set aside time when we intentionally talk with God and listen to each another.

Shortchanging God has not helped me accomplish the things I thought I needed to do any quicker. In fact, when I have taken time to pray, God has helped me set my priorities and given me new insights about the task at hand so that I have actually saved time by taking time to talk with God first. Martin Luther understood this. He said, "I have so much to do today I have to spend four hours in prayer just to get everything done."[1]

Use the following suggestions to begin a plan for daily prayer. Start with ten or fifteen minutes in the morning or whatever time of day you set. Use this time to talk with God and read Scripture. Soon you will find the time so important that you will want to continue beyond your set time. As your prayer life grows, you may stop being a clock-watcher and find that some days you will spend more time in prayer.

When your prayers seem to be going nowhere and you feel the time spent in prayer is boring, listen for God's direction. Review the guidance God has given you in the past. Ask yourself if you have been obedient in following through. It is in obeying that we understand God more intimately, which allows our relationship to grow. The less exciting times may be a signal that we need to change our pattern of praying. Using a variety of prayer styles can keep our prayer lives alive and deepening.

Begin to explore your prayer life by starting where you are comfortable. Søren Kierkegaard once observed, "A man prayed, and at first thought that prayer was talking. But he became more and more quiet until in the end he realized prayer is listening."[2] Some people find that praying is connected to their breathing patterns. As you breathe in, pray words that acknowledge God's presence. As you breathe out, pray words for cleansing. Others find that there are no words to pray. At times like these, simply sitting in silence and listening for God to direct your time together can be very powerful. For some people repeating the name of Jesus over and over is all they can do, and they trust the Spirit to intercede for them. If you are easily distracted when you pray, you may want to kneel beside a chair or focus on some object. You may want to sing your prayers or dance your prayers. Praying is talking with God, and it should be as comfortable as talking with your best friend.

Many of you are pray-ers already. You may have found many different prayer styles that help keep your prayer life fresh. The following are a few prayer styles that I have found particularly helpful at different times in my life.

WRITING YOUR PRAYERS

Bill Hybels introduced me to a very simple, but powerful, style of praying through his book *Too Busy Not to Pray*. He suggests that you take a sheet of paper and divide it into four equal parts. Label each section with one of the following words: Adoration, Confession, Thanksgiving, and Supplication. You will notice that the first letters of these words spell ACTS, an easy way to remember the four categories.

In the first section, write a paragraph giving *adoration* to God. The word adore may not be a part of our everyday vocabulary, but when we come to pray and worship, adoring God is what we are doing. Adoration helps us focus on the One with whom we are talking. It makes us pause to consider who God is. It reminds us of who we are in God's eyes. God tells us to worship and adore him. Look at some of the psalms for examples of adoring God. I often begin by recognizing God's attributes that particularly describe my appreciation for God for that day. Then I move on into situations where I have seen God at work in my life or the lives of others.

Write your *confessions* in the second section. It is easy to say, "God, forgive us for our many sins," and go on with our prayers thinking that we have taken care of that. I invite you, instead, to reflect on your last twenty-four hours. Did you tell a co-worker that you would do something that you didn't even intend to do? Did you exaggerate the number of hours you spent working when you were traveling for business? Or when you filled out your expense account, were you totally honest with the necessary expenditures? You see, you may need to admit to God that you are a liar or that you are cheating. Be honest with God in your confessions. Name the very sin you are wrestling with. Admitting the sin for what it is, whether it is a small thing or something very big, will cleanse your whole being. You will come to understand God's forgiveness and will discover you don't want to continue doing those things that displease God.

The third section is for *thanksgiving*. It is easy to take for granted the many things God does for us every day. I went through a very traumatic experience that left me unable to sleep for more than five minutes at a time for many weeks. The nights got very long. I learned something very important during those trying times. I learned to thank God for faithfully bringing daylight out of darkness. We like to hear people thank us for the little things we do. God likes to hear it, too. Bill Hybels suggests that in our section for Thanksgiving we thank God every day for answered prayers, spiritual blessings, relational blessings, and material blessings. Reflecting in silence on these four areas of life will be restorative.

The last section is *supplication*. After adoring God, confessing our sins, and giving thanks, we are ready to let God know our needs. Bill Hybels has found four categories that help him pray his needs. They are needs that surround his ministry: people in leadership roles, for the unsaved, for the sick in various walks of life, and his family and his personal needs. Find those categories that fit your walk in life and include them as you pray in this section.

When you have completed your written prayer, take it and pray it back to the Lord. You will find that your thoughts while you have been writing pour out as you pray and freshness returns to your prayer life. By writing out your prayer, you also have a way of looking back and seeing how faithful God is to respond to your prayers. [3]

I began using this style of praying at a time when I was distracted and unfocused. I quickly learned that I needed more paper to fill in my needs. I discovered how little I knew about adoring God. I saw how unbalanced my prayer life had become. I learned to keep a pad of paper near my chair where I was praying, and when things would come to my mind that I needed to do, I would write them down. That way I wouldn't forget, but I could lay it aside while keeping my prayer time intact. For me, this method helps when my mind is cluttered and unfocused.

ALLOW SCRIPTURE TO FORM YOU WHEN YOU PRAY

Robert Mulholland, in his book *Shaped by the Word*, says that too often Scripture is read for information. What is needed is to come to Scripture for formation. Come with the attitude that God will shape you through the Word.

Select a short passage of Scripture. The details of the information are not to be the focus. Instead ask yourself several questions such as these:

1. Do you see yourself in any of the people involved in this passage?
2. Had you been present, how would you have reacted?
3. What does God want you to see about yourself in the light of this passage?
4. Ask God to show you more and follow through on what God gives you. Do you need to make a confession? Is there an assignment to be carried out? If you need to go deeper for understanding, take time to do that.

Allowing Scripture to form us is a powerful way to see how our lives may be misguided. It causes us to recognize our attitudes and gives us a basis for opening up important conversations with God. Some passages that might help you begin praying in this manner are Matthew 8:1-4 and Luke 18:9-14. Examples for using this prayer style will be found on pages 127-129.

Put on the whole armor of God every day

At a difficult time in my relationships at work, I began to learn how powerful it is to put on the armor of God each day. We are in a daily battle whether we are aware of it or not. In Ephesians 6:10-11, we are told to "be strong in the Lord and in his mighty power. Put on the full armor of God so that you can take your stand against the devil's schemes." Though many of us do not relate immediately with the language of the armor, we can learn from the example Paul uses. Soldiers each day dress in such a way that they will be protected from harm. Christians need to put on spiritual clothing each day also. It is helpful to get familiar with the elements of the armor for they actually describe the nature of Jesus, who is our salvation, righteousness, and peace. He is truth and the Word of God. Most of the armor has a protective function for vital parts of the body. Only the sword is on the offensive, but how powerful it is. When we combine the Word of God (the sword) with faith (the shield), we have strong protection against the enemy that may try to attack us during the day.

Dian Ginter and Glen Martin, in their book, *Power House*, teach how to put on the armor of God each day.[4] When we put on the *helmet of salvation*, we realize that though we are saved from sin in the past, there is always today for which we need salvation from the power of sin. The helmet protects our minds. Sin originates in the mind. Lying, rebellion, lust, rejection of God, immorality—all begin in the mind before they are carried out.

This prayer style helped me when I was hearing a lot of things that made me feel put down and useless. When I began to pray in this manner, the truth of the situation became clear. I began to take to heart the things that were true and to let the others go without absorbing them. Now, I pray that God will be in control of my thoughts each day. I pray that God will help me discern the things for which I need to use my mind and that I will not absorb all the things I am exposed to through the media, newspapers, and other communication.

The *breastplate of righteousness* protects our hearts. This is the time to pray that we will not shame God, that our lives will be upright in all ways. Pray that God will show you if you are trying to live any other way.

In putting on the *belt of truth*, we ask God to help us understand first of all God's Truth, to bring God's Word to us when we are tempted to compromise our behavior. Ask God to help you always be truthful in your expressions.

It is important to be at peace with God before putting on the *shoes of the gospel of peace*. If you sense turmoil in your relationship with God, reflect on the possibility there may be unconfessed sin in your life. Perhaps you are letting temptations influence your actions. Listen for God to reveal what is causing that unrest and allow your relationship to be restored. Then offer yourself to God to carry peace into difficult situations.

We are often peppered with temptations that are alluring and sometimes so subtle. The *shield of faith* and *the sword of the Spirit* will help us identify those temptations and give us strength to overcome them. Ask God to let your faith be strengthened and to bring to your mind those biblical passages that will speak to your condition. Expect God to give you new insights.

As you conclude this prayer, offer yourself to be a vessel that God can use today. Thank God that you can confidently face the day knowing that God will protect you from the forces of evil that want to invade your life. This is a prayer that can be prayed as you drive to work. It will uplift and equip you for what the day may bring.

KEEP A RECORD OF YOUR PRAYERS AND ANSWERS

Some of us find that keeping a prayer list helps us recall those special concerns that pop up now and then. When we promise to pray for someone, it is important to write that concern on a prayer list so we will follow through. It is also helpful to date when we begin to pray and periodically note when that prayer was answered, or to mark steps along the way as the prayer is being answered. You will be surprised how many times your prayers are answered. Sometimes it may be answered in a way other than you imagined. My experience is that God's ways are always better than my ways. I use a regular notebook with four columns: Initial Date, Prayer Request, Date of Answer, and Answer.

Summary

You have been encouraged to explore your prayer life and venture into some styles that may be refreshing. Begin with what comfortably brings you into that intimate place with God. If it helps you to have a specific prayer corner, use that. If patterning your prayer to the rhythm of your breathing helps bring you into the presence of God, begin with that manner. Bringing variety to your praying often sharpens your prayer time and allows for a richer experience with God. Suggestions for deepening your personal prayer life include writing your prayer using four sections: adoration, confession, thanksgiving, and supplication; allowing scripture to form you as you pray; putting on the whole armor of God; and recording your prayers and answers.

Reflect and Respond

Take time now to experiment with one of these prayer suggestions. Allow God to speak to you as you listen. Expect God to give you new spiritual understanding out of your special times talking with God. You may want to keep a journal as you develop in your experience with prayer.

---

1 Judson Cornwall, *Praying the Scriptures*, used by permission (Lake Mary, FL: Creation House, 1988), pp. 14-15.
2 Søren Kierkegaard, *Christian Discourses*, trans. Walter Lowie (Oxford University Press, 1940) p. 324.
3 Bill Hybels, *Too Busy Not to Pray* (Downers Grove, IL: InterVarsity Press, 1988), pp. 49-60.
4 Glen Martin and Dian Ginter, *Power House* (Nashville, TN: Broadman and Holman, 1994), pp. 131-133. Used by permission.

Other Resource

Robert M. Mulholland Jr., *Shaped By the Word* (Nashville, TN: The Upper Room, 1985).

CHAPTER 3

Maturing in Prayer

Prayer is a relationship between God and the pray-er. As in any relationship—between spouses, friends, or family—there has to be some intentional nurture to keep that relationship alive and growing. God longs to build a growing relationship with us, but sometimes we become content and choose not to become more intimate with God. Communication is one of the best ways to keep a human relationship growing. The same is true of our relationship with God. We communicate with God through prayer. We also communicate by doing the things God teaches us to do.

As we listen to people pray, we may appreciate their eloquence in choice of words. We may quietly say in our hearts that we can never pray like that person. On other occasions, we may feel that our prayers become very repetitious and uninteresting. We find ourselves backing off from praying. Consider what happens when we talk with our best friend. We don't worry about what other people will say. God wants to be our best friend and invites us to be at ease in those conversations. God will hear and understand our hearts. Our relationship with God will grow through developing our prayer life.

No one is born a prayer hero. Prayer heroes are shaped and refined through practice and experience. Prayer is not something we observe from afar; it is an activity in which people must participate. Skills are developed as we actually pray. In their book, *Power House*, Dian Ginter and Glen Martin suggest that there are several levels to be experienced as one's prayer life matures.[1] Each level builds on the one before, just as math builds on addition and subtraction and continues to expand into more complex understanding. The newer levels may be more advanced and complex in their application of the older truths, but they still rely on the foundations of the preceding levels. Just as we do with math, we will sometimes use the simpler skills in prayer while other times we will need to call on the more advanced skills.

A relationship with God that is growing will move and expand as we experience more and allow God to lead us into new depths. See where you are in the following levels and explore the greater possibilities God offers you to grow in your understanding.

Level 1: Introduction. When we discover that we can talk with God over matters that concern us both, our prayer life is at its first level. Prayers will be focused mostly on the things that affect us. Characteristic words will be "give me," help me," "protect me," "solve my problems." We recognize a need and acknowledge that prayer is valuable. For many, the concept of prayer at this stage is that God is like a puppet. We ask. God should respond accordingly. Prayer may not come too naturally at this stage. It may almost feel like a burden but as in learning to play the piano, practice is required. To develop your prayer life, begin by setting aside a few minutes a day when you talk with God. Take time to listen to what God has to teach you about himself and about prayer. When you begin to ask God to help you have a greater burden for the things God wants to see accomplished, you will move on to the next level in the growth process.

Level 2: Concern beyond self. When we get to know someone, we want to have other friends meet this person. As our prayer life develops, we will want to include others as we talk with God. We move beyond our very self-oriented prayer to including others—our church, our friends, co-workers, those who are serving God in other cultures. Teachings from Scripture become a guide for our prayers. For example 1 Timothy 2:1-4 says "I urge, then, first of all, that requests, prayers, intercession and thanksgiving be made for everyone—for kings and all those in authority, that we may live peaceful and quiet lives in all godliness and holiness. This is good, and pleases God our Savior, who wants all [people] to be saved and to come to a knowledge of the truth." As you face different issues in the various facets of life, you will find yourself including those concerns in your prayers. For example, when there is turmoil within society, pray for those who have authority to make a difference. You will also care about those who haven't yet come into a relationship with Jesus and pray for them.

Verses like Romans 8:28 will have fresh meaning. "And we know that in all things God works for the good of those who love him, who have been called according to his purpose."

A few years ago I took a visitor from Kenya back to the airport to meet his plane to return to his home country. For some reason, unknown to us, his ticket had been cancelled. No flight was available for him for two days. His comment as we got in the car caught my attention. "God, you have promised to work everything out for good. I don't see how this can turn out for good. You're in control. I trust you." The next two days he spent with a Kenyan family living in America. He realized that his visit to them was important for they needed encouragement and a touch from their own people.

God will use a variety of ways to help us move on to the next level if we keep alert to God's involvement in our lives.

Level 3: Learning from others. As we become more focused on praying, we notice a lot more about how others pray. I love to hear people from the developing countries pray. They pray with such insight and faith. It is so natural to them to turn to God. Often times, they refer to God's Word in their prayers. They remind God of promises that have been given. They accept their plight and faults like David does in the Psalms. Their prayers are much more God-centered than self-centered.

It is in this stage that you may find yourself compelled to do some study in the area of prayer. You may choose to read books on the subject or share discussions on prayer in small study groups or attend seminars on prayer. Prayer is a subject that never seems to get exhausted because there is always more to learn.

While in Kenya, I had the occasion to teach in the Bible School on our Friends mission. It was during a December holiday that I sensed God's invitation to spend two hours a day in prayer. I certainly believed in prayer, but I have to admit that praying daily for two hours was not a habit of mine at that time. I wondered how I would manage it, especially when I realized that there would be visitors coming from various places in the world. Hotels were far away and expensive, so it was important that we make room in our homes for the flow of visitors. Cooking was a challenge. No frozen foods, cake mixes or prepared foods were affordable, even if they were available. We began food preparations by boiling and filtering extra water for drinking. We started with peas in the pod. Everything had to be prepared from scratch. These visitors had things they wanted to see and do, which meant that someone had to work out those plans and often accompany them. It seemed like an impossible thing to find two uninterrupted hours with God daily. Finding alone space would be tricky, too, because not only did the living room turn into wall-to-wall mattresses at night, it was imperative to set up a cot in my bedroom to accommodate the visitors.

Shortly before that holiday time began, a friend gave me a book by Dick Eastman called *The Hour That Changes the World*. As I studied that book, I began to see that there was so much more to prayer than I was experiencing. My heart yearned to venture out in my prayer life. Those two hours I committed to prayer did not seem long. They were very precious times. God helped me find not only the time each day but God revealed to me things I had never known before. It was truly a growing time for me.

Many times at this level of maturity, we find ourselves willing to experiment with a variety of prayer forms. Journaling, praying the words of scripture, singing prayers, or using a variety of postures for praying all may be helpful. As you experience new approaches, your prayer horizons will broaden and your relationship with the Lord will be strengthened.

We must never become content and think we have achieved all there is to know about prayer, for there is more. God wants to share his heart with us. A friend was talking with me about his marriage on one occasion. He commented that he always thought he and his wife had an unusually good relationship but he noticed that it was even getting better. God doesn't want our relationship to be stagnant. There is always more to learn and experiences from which to grow.

Level 4: Intercession. Intercession is coming to God on behalf of another. It is a part of the earlier prayer levels, but at this stage, prayer offered on behalf of others now is both a burden and a desire. We feel almost compelled to pray. As we pray, we find we want to spend more time with God and bring the concerns laid on our hearts for another. We find delight in God. What is happening is that we are feeling what our Intimate Friend feels about these situations. Prayer is the natural outflow as we ask God to give us understanding for the situation—to help us see the situation from God's perspective. We have moved a long way from focusing on ourselves. It no longer feels such a burden. We see God's power being released as we pray, and our faith becomes stronger.

Level 5: Pray with growing faith. At this level, there is no doubt in our minds that God is a God who hears and answers prayer. We are willing to reach for greater things as we talk with God—things that require us to rely on God, things that we know cannot be achieved by our own abilities.

Sometimes these leaps of faith are on a fairly simple scale. I mentioned earlier that I was sent to M. D. Anderson Cancer Center for a second opinion for the treatment of my newly diagnosed cancer. When I was told that I should join the study and plan to stay in Houston for five months, I was overwhelmed with making that decision. I was given two days to decide if I should choose the option offered. There were so many things to consider. Would insurance cover the expenses? What would happen about my job? Where would I stay? Who would stay with me? The night before I had to give an answer to the doctor, I did something I seldom do. I told God I needed a sign so I would know the right thing to do. I had no idea what "sign" God could put together by nine o'clock the next morning, but I fell asleep trusting. The next morning, as was my custom, I started the day reading my Bible using the aid of a devotional book. Some additional references were suggested in the context of the reading. I began to browse through those suggested readings. Suddenly, three words stood out from the page: "...Now choose life..." (Deuteronomy 30:19). In that instant I knew that God was giving me the answer. I was to choose life and arrange to stay in Houston for treatment.

When we experience God caring about the seemingly small things such as these, we know we can trust God for much greater things. At this stage, we may seek out a friend who will be willing to pray with us on a regular basis. Sharing together in prayer allows for discovering new insights about prayer. Our prayers will have a greater breadth and depth to them.

It is possible to plateau at any one level or to move back and forth between the different levels but there is still more! To experience the next level, we need to be very in tune with God. You may want to be intentional about walking with people for whom God has unlocked the truths of invasion.

Level 6: Pray against the enemy. This level moves us into the arena of spiritual warfare. This term may be unfamiliar. Paul helps explain it in Ephesians 6:12: "For our struggle is not against flesh and blood, but against the rulers, against the authorities, against the powers of this dark world and against the spiritual forces of evil in the heavenly realms."

In his book *Churches that Pray*, Peter Wagner describes this activity. "What Paul may not have known then, but later learned through experience, was that when Satan has unbelievers under his control, he does not give them up without a fight. This is what we now call spiritual warfare."[2] He then quotes Clinton E. Arnold who says that "The primary aggressive action the Christian is called to take in the world is to spread the gospel" and the principal weapon of spiritual warfare that will be needed as we move into the evangelization of our community is prayer.[3]

Discernment given by God is sharpened at this level and we become aware of the spiritual struggles that are going on between the power of evil and the power of God. We are given insights to know when and how to pray in the power of Jesus against the evil. We will sense the grieving of the Spirit over things and issues that are going on around us. We have a greater sense of God's power and authority flowing through us as we pray.

Satan fears prayer more than any other ministry, so when we pray against evil that is controlled by Satan, it is not unusual to see the struggle before evil is overcome. The darkness of sin becomes much more painful. When we face opposition within these struggles, we know where it is coming from and will need to persist in prayer.

Summary

Prayer is a relationship between God and the pray-er. That relationship has to be nurtured to keep it alive. Prayer provides that opportunity. Our life of prayer develops through various stages. Though we build on each stage, we may flow from one stage to another at different times. The levels identified are as follows.

1. In the Introduction level, we experience a need and somehow know that prayer is available to us. Our prayers will be very self-focused.
2. Concern Beyond Ourselves is the next level, where we want to extend our prayers to include concerns such as the church, those who are serving God in different cultures, the social ills in society, and those in positions to make a difference about the social ills.
3. Continuing to grow in our prayer life, we notice how others pray so the third stage is called Learning from Others. This is a time when we listen to others pray. We are interested in reading books on the subject or sharing prayer experiences in small groups or attending prayer seminars that help us understand prayer. We may experiment with a variety of prayer forms such

as journaling, singing, praying the Scripture, changing our posture.
4. Intercession, though a part of all the stages, now takes on greater significance as we not only feel driven to pray for another but we discover more clearly how our Intimate Friend feels about the situation.
5. As we see the power of prayer played out, our faith is increased and we are willing to ask God for things we know we cannot achieve by ourselves. The fifth stage is Praying with Growing Faith.
6. Praying Against the Enemy is the stage that will bring us into the area of spiritual warfare where we are given discernment to identify the struggle occurring between evil and the power of God.

REFLECT AND RESPOND

Pause for a moment and quietly listen as God leads you into a deeper understanding of prayer. Consider which levels of prayer you have already experienced. Ask God to teach you more and to give you a desire to have a more vital prayer life. Is there someone with whom you can share times of praying to help you grow in your prayer life?

---

1 Glen Martin and Dian Ginter, *Power House* (Nashville, TN: Broadman and Holman Publishers, 1994), pp. 97-107. Used by permission.
2 Peter Wagner, *Churches That Pray* (Ventura, CA: Regal Books, 1993), p. 133.
3 Ibid., p. 134.

Other Resources
   Dick Eastman, *The Hour That Changes the World* (Grand Rapids, MI: Baker Book House, 1978).

CHAPTER 4

A Biblical Prayer Teaches Interactive Skills

We have defined prayer; we have looked at why we should pray and how we can mature in prayer. Now let's examine one of the prayers from the Bible to gain some helpful insights about praying. The Bible records at least 650 definite prayers of which 450 have recorded answers. These prayers are rich resources to teach praying effectively. In Exodus 32—33, Moses and God have an important interaction. As we look closely at this prayer, watch for aspects that can strengthen your prayers.

Moses had just concluded the glorious session with God on Mount Sinai where he received the Ten Commandments. Surely this experience had given Moses confidence to continue leading the people. Those commandments provided guidelines for interacting with one another and worshipping God. Moses had been away a long time from the people he was leading. He was eager to share those commandments with them.

GOD INITIATES PRAYER.

As he prepared to descend the mountain, Moses busied himself collecting the few things he had taken with him. He heard the Lord speaking urgently to him, "Go down, because your people, whom you brought up out of Egypt, have become corrupt" (32:7). Had Moses heard right? Did God really call these people his [Moses'] people? Always in their conversations God had referred to these people as God's people.

There was no time to ponder this issue for God continued to speak and Moses didn't want to miss anything that God was saying. "...they have been quick to turn away from what I commanded them and have made themselves an idol cast in the shape of a calf. They have bowed down to it and sacrificed to it and have said, 'These are your gods, O Israel, who brought you up out of Egypt'" (32:8).

God continued to speak against the people, "I have seen this people, and they are a stiff-necked people" (32:9). Moses' mind was in turmoil. Had God disowned these people? Moses remembered all that had happened to bring them to this place. God had chosen these oppressed slave people to be his people. It was God who had visited Moses and called him to lead these people where they would never have gone by themselves. How could God think of abandoning them at this point?

Moses didn't have time to ponder these questions for God was still speaking. "Now leave me alone so that my anger may burn against them, and that I may destroy them. Then I will make you into a great nation" (32:10).

PRAYER MAY CHALLENGE OUR BELIEFS.

Moses must have thought it would be a relief to get rid of this undisciplined mob and start building a great nation from him and his family as God offered. But he realized that he was facing a crisis. His whole understanding of God was being challenged. His role in the course of events was left dangling. He had grown to love those people and now he was being torn between two incompatible loves: his love for God and his love for the people he was leading to the Promised Land.

Moses remembered the power of God he had seen demonstrated. He first recalled his own private experience when God called him out of the burning bush. As he had led the people, over and over they had witnessed God's power. God divided the Red Sea when mountains and the sea blocked them and Pharaoh's army was hot on their trail. They had walked across on dry land. God had provided food and water in unexpected ways.

PRAYER IS A TWO-WAY CONVERSATION.

There was no time to reminisce. Moses must face the present with boldness. Moses would have to address God in a very straightforward manner. God must hear Moses' side of this story.

PRAYER INVITES BOLDNESS IN BARING OUR HEARTS TO GOD.

"O Lord, why should your anger burn against your people whom you brought out of Egypt with great power and a mighty hand? Why should the Egyptians say, 'It was with evil intent that he brought them out, to kill them in the mountains and to wipe them off the face of the earth'? Turn from your fierce anger; relent and do not bring disaster on your people. Remember your servants Abraham, Isaac and Israel, to whom you swore by your own self: 'I will make your descendants as numerous as the stars in the sky and I will give your descendants all this land I promised them, and it will be their inheritance forever'" (32:11-13).

This was no "God bless our church. Amen" type of prayer. Moses boldly confronted God with the promises God had made to these people.

Prayer is God-centered.

It would seem appropriate from our viewpoint for Moses to say, "Now what, God? You've made me leave my flocks and put me to this heavy task of leading these people out of bondage only to abandon us. What about me? What am I supposed to do? How will these people survive?" But that's not at all what Moses did. Two things dominated his prayer: 1) the tender concern for the nation he was leading and 2) the passionate jealousy for the reputation of God.[1]

Prayer is presenting God with our concerns.

Moses wanted to find some way to restore this relationship between God and the people. After all, God made the covenant agreement that he would be the God of these people and the Israelites would be his people. How could God back down from that without losing his reputation? Moses remembered the need to keep God's name holy and trustworthy.

Prayer can change God's plans.

God was moved when he heard Moses' prayer. "Then the Lord relented and did not bring on his people the disaster he had threatened" (32:14).

Moses, a bit shaken, picked up the tablets and started down the mountain. In one sense he was relieved that God had relented, but he now faced the uncertainty of what was ahead. Moses heard an unidentifiable noise. When the people came into view, he found them dancing around the calf—just as God had said. Now it was Moses' anger that burned. The truth of what God said sank in very deeply.

Moses asked Aaron for an explanation. Aaron's response only twisted the truth. There was no time to deal with Aaron. Moses had to confront the people with the dire sin they had committed. Boldly, Moses called the people into account. Moses knew that reconciliation would be required between the people and God. The sin they had committed was so bad that at last Moses told them that he would "go up to the Lord; perhaps I can make atonement for your sin" (32:30).

PRAYER IS INTENDED TO BE A PLACE FOR SHARING AND TAKING COUNSEL WITH GOD ON MATTERS OF IMPORTANCE TO GOD.

Moses sought out a place where he could hold a private dialogue with God. With hunched shoulders, he walked slowly. Perhaps he said, "You were right, God. What a great sin these people have committed! They have made themselves gods of gold" (32:31). Then with determination, he came to the point of this prayer: "But now, please forgive their sin...." (32:32a). Then with less assurance, he added, "but if not, then blot me out of the book you have written" (32:32b).

PRAYER BRINGS US TO A POINT OF SUBMISSION.

Moses had come to the point of absolute selflessness. His desire for God to forgive the people was greater than what it might cost him. He was willing to let go of any predetermined response from God and accept the answer God would give.

PRAYER REQUIRES OBEDIENCE TO FOLLOW GOD'S COMMANDS.

God's response probably wasn't exactly what Moses expected. "Whoever has sinned against me I will blot out of my book" (32:33). He's making it clear to Moses that God alone determines whose names remain in the book. Moses' task was to "lead the people to the place I spoke of, and my angel will go before you" (32:34).

Moses felt relieved that his task was to continue as the leader of these people but he wanted to be perfectly clear with God that the relationship would be right. He said, "You have been telling me, 'Lead these people,' but you have not let me know whom you will send with me. You have said, 'I know you by name and you have found favor with me. If I have found favor in your eyes, teach me your ways so I may know you and continue to find favor with you. Remember that this nation is your people" (33:12-13).

The Lord was tender toward Moses as he replied, "My Presence will go with you, and I will give you rest" (33:14). Moses' confidence was returning but there was one more thing Moses had to know. "If your Presence does not go with us, do not send us up from here. How will anyone know that you are pleased with me and with your people unless you go with us? What else will distinguish me and your people from all the other people on the face of the earth?" (33:15-16).

PRAYER IS EXPERIENCING GOD'S LOVE FOR US.

The Lord responded, "I will do the very thing you have asked, because I am pleased with you and I know you by name" (33:17). This dialogue between Moses and God gives us a glimpse into several aspects of prayer that can be applied in our prayers. You may note other important aspects in this prayer.

SUMMARY

This prayer of Moses, found in Exodus 32-33, teaches many things about dialoguing with God. Consider your interaction with God as you reflect on these insights.

1. God initiates prayer.
2. Prayer may challenge our beliefs or our perceptions of God. This requires the exercise of our faith and adjustment of our life to accommodate the new leading or teaching.
3. Prayer is a two-way conversation. God wants to hear our hearts, and God listens carefully. We must also listen to God for understanding and direction.
4. Prayer invites boldness in baring our hearts to God. God can handle our anger and hurts. God wants us to be honest in sharing our feelings and concerns.
5. Prayer should be God-centered.
6. Prayer is presenting God with our concerns and being willing to accept God's responses even when they differ from our expectations.
7. Prayer can change God's plans.
8. Prayer is intended to be a sharing and taking counsel with God on matters of importance to God.

9. Prayer brings us to a point of submission where we are more desirous of fulfilling God's plan than manipulating things to happen like we perceive they should.
10. Prayer requires obedience on our part. In obeying, our faith grows and our prayer life becomes mature.
11. Prayer is experiencing God's love for us. When we find that place of understanding and caring, there is a peace that God gives out of an expression of love for us.

REFLECT AND RESPOND

Reflect on this learning from Moses. Compare to your prayer experience. Are there times when your beliefs have been challenged? Do you know the joy that comes when you lay aside your predetermined expectations and accept God's responses? Would you say your prayers are God-centered? Do you know God's love for you?

---

1 John White, *Daring to Draw Near* (Downers Grove, IL: InterVarsity Press, 1977), p.40.

CHAPTER 5

Praying with the Lord's Prayer

There are times when it is hard to know how to pray. Maybe you've been asked to pray for someone who was going through a tough experience and as you began to pray you realized that you really didn't know how to pray for the situation. The Bible gives guidance and vocabulary for times like these.

A few years ago, friends of mine asked me to pray for their son whose marriage was about to result in separation. I knew this son and his family, but not well. I certainly knew little about the cause of their disharmony. When I began to pray, my prayer seemed no more than words. How could I pray more effectively for this situation?

I began looking in my Bible for passages where God's expectations for marriage were laid out. I discovered a language to pray for my friends' children. Passages such as Ephesians 5:22-33 and 1 Corinthians 7:1-7 became very helpful as I began asking God to help this couple to devote themselves to prayer as they worked through their differences. I prayed that their love for each other would be pure and whole, that they would be faithful to each other as they remembered

Christ's faithfulness to his bride, the church. Using the words of Scripture brought life and purpose in my own prayers for this couple.

The disciples reached a similar place in their desire to know more about praying. Luke 11:1 says that one disciple came to Jesus and said, "Lord, teach us to pray." Jesus' response was to give them a model prayer known today as the Lord's Prayer. It wasn't until I realized the outline of the prayer that it came to enhance my own prayer life in very special ways. We will look at Matthew 6:9-13.

"OUR FATHER, IN HEAVEN" (V. 9).

Notice that the prayer begins with a focus on God: "Our Father in heaven…." It recognizes God as a being with whom we can relate. It begins an intimate conversation with someone who cares about us, who provides for us, who created us, and who responds to us. The fact that we can approach God directly is very special. By acknowledging that God is in heaven, we are aware also that God is the God of the universe. We may feel that God couldn't care about us when he is overseeing the whole universe. But God has the capacity beyond human comprehension to care about each of us while watching over the whole universe. God loves us and longs for an intimate relationship with each person.

"HALLOWED BE YOUR NAME" (V. 9).

"Hallowed" is not a word often used in our vocabulary. The word actually comes from the Greek word *hagiazo*, which means "to be holy." In this prayer then, we are essentially saying, "Our Father in heaven, Your name is holy." This gives the opportunity to adore and praise God, to think about the many names of God and consider the characteristics that each name embraces. David Jeremiah, in his book *Prayer, The Great Adventure* reminds us of some of the names of God.

Yahweh Tsidkenu	The Lord who Sanctifies
Yahweh Shalom	The Lord who is our Peace
Yahweh Shammah	The Lord is there, he never leaves us
Yahweh Rophe	The Lord who heals
Yahweh Jireh	The Lord who provides
Yahweh Nissi	The Lord my Banner
Yahweh Rohi	The Lord who is my Shepherd

Suppose we come to God with a problem of sin. Using this prayer model, we want to acknowledge that aspect of God's character that can meet this need. We might want to recognize the holiness of God by using Yahweh Tsidkenu, the Lord, our Righteousness. Perhaps someone is ill, and in talking with God, you see that characteristic of God as Healer and you call on Yahweh Rophe.[1] Using the names of God will personalize our relationship with God. Our conversation will go to a deeper level.

Opening our prayer in this manner brings us to God with praise, adoration and worship. It helps us to focus our prayer on God rather than on ourselves. It positions us to move to the next part where we look to God for our priorities.

"YOUR KINGDOM COME, YOUR WILL BE DONE ON EARTH AS IT IS IN HEAVEN" (V.10).

God lives in our hearts if we have invited God in. Expressing this part of the prayer essentially says that we want God's principles and purposes to be lived out within us while God reigns within. We want to know God's will so our priorities will be in order. Society tries to dictate something different. It tries to say that we are in control of our lives and we don't have to submit ourselves to anyone—not even God. For me, submitting to God's principles and purposes is an act of love, not a hardship of submission. I long to be available to God for use in accomplishing God's purposes. That may mean that I have to make some adjustments in what I do, but I do them gladly out of love for God. Setting priorities during our prayer time can help us be more aware of God's purposes as we go about our daily activities.

Sometimes we may sense God's nudging to do something that seems very insignificant. The easy thing may be to ignore that guidance. It really is our responsibility, however, to obey and leave the results to God. This story of a missionary doctor working with the Overseas Missionary Fellowship bears this out.

A missionary doctor in Africa made routine trips from his field hospital into a nearby city for supplies. The distance was such that he had to camp overnight. On one of these visits to the city, he saw two men fighting. One was injured, so he treated him and witnessed to him about the Lord Jesus Christ. He then returned home without incident.

On his next trip to the city, he ran into the man who had been injured. The man told him that he and some friends, who knew that he was carrying money and medicines, had followed him to his campsite as he had left the city, planning to kill and rob him.

"Just as we were about to attack you, we saw that you were surrounded by twenty-six armed guards, so we went away in fear," said the man.

The missionary assured the man that he had camped alone, but the man was adamant that his friends had seen the guards also, and had counted them. There were twenty-six.

Several months later, the missionary told that story in his home church in Michigan. In the middle of the story, a man in the congregation rose and asked the date of the incident. When the missionary finally recalled the date, the man said that on that very date he had felt such a strong urge to pray for the missionary that he had left the golf course and had called several men of the church together to pray for him. It was daytime in Michigan, and nighttime in Africa.

"In fact," said the man, "the men who prayed with me are in this room." He then asked the men to stand. As they stood one by one to join the man, the missionary counted. There were twenty-six men.

How easy it would have been for the golfer to say that it didn't make any sense to delay his trip to the golf course when he didn't have a clue why that nudging to pray for the medical missionary was important. Thank God, he was a person who let God's purposes take priority.

Henry Blackaby, in his book *Experiencing God*, puts in a nutshell what praying for "God's will to be done on earth as it is in heaven" really does. He says that we agree with God that we will follow God one day at a time; agree to follow God even when the details are not totally defined; agree that we will let God be our Way.[2]

From this model prayer of Jesus, by beginning our prayer focusing on God and choosing to align our lives with God's will, we are prepared to move on to praying for ourselves.

You will be surprised to see how you look at your needs differently when you begin by acknowledging God, taking time to reflect on the various characteristics of God, and considering what God's priorities may be.

"GIVE US TODAY OUR DAILY BREAD" (V. 11).
Acknowledge your own needs and recognize that God is the Provider. Begin to let God know your basic needs such as food, shelter, clothing, and work. Notice though, that Jesus doesn't limit it to "you." In other words, even as we express our needs, we think of what is best for those around us as well. That may help us put a healthier slant on how to pray for our needs.

As we talk with God about our needs, we can expect our faith to be challenged and strengthened. Henry Blackaby tells the story of faith as friends of his laid their needs before God. In his church in Saskatoon, there was the sense that God wanted them to start new churches throughout Saskatchewan. They felt led to call a man by the name of Len Koster to become their minister of mission outreach. Len had had fourteen years of experience as a pastor. He had served those pastorates as a bi-vocational pastor. During those years, he and his wife saved $7,000 hoping that some day they would be able to purchase their own home.

When the Kosters felt God's call to start the churches, there was no money available to help them move or provide a salary. Len Koster's response was, "Henry, the God who has called me will help me. We will take the money from our savings, and we will move." Later he told Henry that he and his wife felt the need to start new churches was so great that they must do it full time and not expect to do it bi-vocationally. As they prayed and talked it over, they realized that the $7,000 they had in the bank was God's, and they were willing to use it to live on. They trusted God to show them how to live when it was gone. They were confident God would provide their support.

Two days later a letter came from a Presbyterian layman in Kamloops, British Columbia. The man wrote that he understood that Len Koster had come to work with them and that God had laid on his heart that he was to support that ministry. Enclosed was a check for $7,000.

When Henry talked with Len he said, "Len, you have placed your life savings on the altar of sacrifice, but God has something else in the bushes. The God who says, 'I am your Provider' has just provided!" What a witness to God's power to provide! How the faith of the church grew. They knew they could step out by faith and God would provide. That experience helped them all learn how to trust God.[3]

Talking with God about our needs must include knowing confidently what God wants to do and trusting God to provide in God's own way and time.

"Forgive us our debts, as we also have forgiven our debtors" (v. 12).

Some translations for this read, "forgive us our sins, for we ourselves forgive everyone indebted to us" (Luke 11:4 NRSV). Let's consider our relationships. Are they all intact? Consider first your relationship with God. Is there anything you need to confess to him? Are you holding a grudge toward someone you are working with, someone in your family, someone in your church? Talk with God about those relationships. By God's grace, you can forgive that person who may have wronged you. You can confess the error of your own way if you are reminded of something you have done that grieves someone else. In reviewing your relationships in God's presence, you will know when an action needs to be initiated to right the wrong. Maybe you will need to find the occasion to talk with someone or write a note of apology. Release comes when you take the necessary steps to put your personal relationships in order.

"AND LEAD US NOT INTO TEMPTATION, BUT DELIVER US FROM THE EVIL ONE" (V. 13).

We are seeking God's protection as we pray this part of the prayer. God will never lead us into temptation, but God knows that in the world we will encounter temptations. Temptations can lure us off track into sin. So ask God to give you strength and courage to remain true to God's will. The forces of evil can easily distract us. Name those things that weigh you down such as fears, phobias, and feelings of persecution. As you pray for protection, ask God to deliver you from the adversarial things that try to claim your attention and distort your sense of God's love and care. God is able to protect you from being drawn into the webs of evil.

We come now to the last part of the Lord's Prayer:

FOR THINE IS THE KINGDOM AND THE POWER AND THE GLORY FOREVER.

Notice how the focus returns to God who promises eternal life. Acknowledge God's power that is involved in energizing the world, and give praise for God's glory and majesty.

Praying through the Lord's Prayer in this manner allows our prayer to be more whole. The focus is clearer. Priorities can be determined through God's perspectives. Needs are more carefully defined. We come away from prayer feeling closer to God, cleaner in heart, and clearer in purpose.

SUMMARY

Praying with the Scripture can enhance our prayer life immensely. In this chapter, the Lord's Prayer has given a model outline for personal prayer experience.

1. Emphasis on God;
   a. Praise (Matthew 6:9).
   b.   Priorities (Matthew 6:10).
2. Emphasis on us.
   a. Provision (Matthew 6:11).
   b. Personal relationships (Matthew 6:12).
   c. Protection (Matthew 6:13a).
3. Emphasis on God's promises (Matthew 6:13b).[4]

REFLECT AND RESPOND

For the next five minutes, try praying with the outline of Jesus' model prayer. When you finish, take time to consider how that experience was for you. Did you find that you felt closer to God, cleaner in your heart and clearer in your purpose? Find someone with whom you can discuss this experience.

1. David Jeremiah, *Prayer, The Great Adventure* (Sisters, OR: Multnomah Publishers, Inc., 1997), p. 93.
2. Henry Blackaby and Claude V. King, *Experiencing God* (Nashville, TN: Broadman and Holman Publishers, 1994), p. 23.
3. Ibid., p. 114-115.
4. Jeremiah, Ibid., pp. 69-190.

Other Resources

Paul Cedar, *A Life of Prayer,* Nashville (TN: Word Publishing, 1998).
Max Lucado, *The Great House of God* (Dallas, TX: Word Publishing, 1997).

CHAPTER 6

Praying for Others

People sometimes ask why they need to pray. They argue that God knows what is needed before they ask anyway, so why do they need to talk to God. I believe it is God's choice to work on earth through people, not independent of them. For God's purposes to be accomplished, God needs to communicate with people who desire to see God's plans fulfilled.

The life of Daniel in the Old Testament helps us understand this concept. In 606 B.C., Judah had been taken captive by another nation because of its sin. Years later, Daniel was reading from the prophet Jeremiah (Daniel 9). He read about the time of captivity that was going to come to the Israelite people and recognized that indeed he was living in that time. As he continued to read he discovered that Jeremiah not only prophesied the captivity, but he also prophesied how long that captivity would last—seventy years. As Daniel calculated the time, he realized that seventy years were nearly over.

Now some people would have read that and sat back passively waiting to see what would happen. But Daniel was different. Daniel knew that God needed his involvement. Listen to what he says in Daniel 9:3. "So I turned to the Lord God and pleaded with him in prayer and petition, in fasting, and in sackcloth and ashes."

The angel Gabriel was dispatched immediately after Daniel started praying but it took twenty-one days to penetrate the warfare in the heavens with the message to inform Daniel that "your words were heard, and I have come in response to them" (Daniel 10:12).

What Daniel realized is that intercession had a part to play in bringing Jeremiah's prophecy to pass. God had made the prophecy. When it was time for its fulfillment God did not fulfill it arbitrarily. God sought for a person upon whose heart he could lay a burden of intercession. That person was Daniel. His role was to enforce that decision on earth through intercession and faith.

Intercession. Though a very old term, many people ask what it means. Some will tell me that all prayer is a form of intercession. I qualify that statement by saying that all intercession is prayer but there are other forms of prayer. For example, praise is a form of prayer; repentance is another form of prayer; relinquishment is yet another form of prayer. So what is intercession or intercessory prayer? Very simply defined, it is "coming to God on behalf of another." Cindy Jacobs, in her training manual for intercession uses a definition that I like. She says that an "intercessor is one with whom God shares his secrets to cover in prayer." [1]

Intercession is modeled for us over and over in the Scriptures. For example, the prayer of Moses, which we looked at in chapter 4, is a prayer of intercession (Exodus 32-33). When Esther called people to fast and pray before she risked her life to confront the king with his decree that would destroy the Jewish people, she was asking them to intercede for her (Esther 4-5). Jesus prayed a powerful prayer of intercession for the disciples, the early church, and even for us in John 17. The early church exercised intercessory prayer when Peter was imprisoned (Acts 12).

At some time we come to God in prayer on behalf of another. We may have prayed for someone who was ill and asked for healing, for our pastor, or for someone going through a rough time. There are people who seem to have a special gift in intercessory prayer. They pray for extended periods of time on a regular basis and see frequent and specific answers to their prayers to a degree much greater than that of the average Christian.

These people are called out to stand in the gap before God on behalf of another. They have a very close relationship with God and enjoy spending much time with God in prayer. One contemporary intercessor takes joy in praying for church leaders. He feels that he participates with them in their ministries and thus receives the blessing of the fruits of their ministries. The exciting thing is that people for whom others are praying become very aware that their ministries are stronger because of the prayers genuinely lifted to God on their behalf.

Peter Wagner helps bring understanding about intercessors in his book *Prayer Shield*. He identifies four types of intercessors, each of whom has a very important role to play.

They are identified as general intercessors, personal intercessors, crisis intercessors and warfare intercessors.[2]

GENERAL INTERCESSORS

Is there someone in your church you turn to when you are having problems? What is it that elicits your trust in them? It is possible that they are general intercessors. You know they will take your concern seriously. They will pray. They will keep praying until God brings an answer. They are likely to keep in touch with you and genuinely walk with you until peace comes. These people don't mind spending long hours praying over prayer lists, prayer guides, and any number of miscellaneous prayer requests given to them.

PERSONAL INTERCESSORS

There are other people who respond to a special calling to pray on a regular and intense basis for a specific person(s). Very often that person to be prayed for is a pastor or Christian leader. Christian leaders are often targets of the evil one. They need to be upheld so when temptation comes, they have strength to overcome.

In those churches where people have come forward and become a personal intercessor for their pastor, they will tell you that their churches have become much stronger. Personal intercessors will usually keep aware of the activities, ministries, and needs of the person for whom they are called to pray. This awareness helps them to pray more specifically. Sometimes God will give them insights into a problem the recipient of their prayers is facing. They may be given words of encouragement or direction to share with the leader for whom they are called to pray. Sometimes the personal intercessor has been made aware of danger in which their leader has been placed. They know to pray for protection during such a crisis. Remarkable things have occurred because these people pray, sometimes altering major decisions for the church or the person for whom they are praying.

Paul understood the need to have personal intercessors. He mentions them from time to time in his writings: 1 Thessalonians 5:25; Romans 15:30; 2 Corinthians 1:11; Philippians 1:19. In all of these references, Paul acknowledges the importance he places on people interceding for him. The most under-used source of spiritual power in churches today is intercession for Christian leaders.

Your calling may be to pray faithfully for your Sunday school teacher, the elders in your church, your pastor. Don't be surprised as you see exciting things take place. Acknowledge from whence those things come.

CRISIS INTERCESSORS

Crisis intercessors will not find praying over lists very compelling. Their experience is to respond to an urgent assignment to pray for someone in dire need. They know the assignment comes from God. They may not know exactly what is happening but they find it impossible to stop praying until the crisis is resolved and they are given peace. Some of these assignments may continue over a long period of time, while others may be short term.

In 1993 as I slept on the night before Easter, I was suddenly awakened with a man on top of me. I was blindfolded. My mouth was taped shut. My hands and feet were tied in such a way I was unable to move. He threatened to stab me. I was raped. My hands and feet turned black as the ties occluded the circulation and damaged the nerves. In the darkness of that night I felt terror as I had never felt before. Yet I never felt abandoned by God. In those sixteen hours before anyone found me, I prayed that the visitors I had invited for dinner on Easter evening would not leave when I didn't answer the door, but that they would somehow know something was wrong and do something about it.

Little did I know what God was doing. It wasn't until about two weeks later that I learned that the night of my attack, a Friends pastor in a little church about three hours away from where I lived had been awakened at the very time the serial rapist was assaulting me. All this pastor knew was that he must pray for me, and that he did. He continued to pray as he went to his Easter service and, not feeling released, invited his church to join him in praying for me even though it was unknown what the problem was. I learned that five people vocalized very sincere and concerned prayers for me. Those prayers, I believe, sustained me during those long, lonely hours as I watched my hands and feet turn black. I was certain that gangrene was setting in. By the grace of God, however, my hands and feet were preserved and with months of therapy, I have regained full use of my extremities. How I thank God for faithful intercessors!

Warfare Intercessors

Though people resist the idea of spiritual warfare, it is important to acknowledge that the forces of evil work hard to overcome the forces of good. God's power is stronger than the evil, but evil tries to take over in many parts of our lives. Warfare intercessors are those who are called to engage the enemy in high-level spiritual warfare.

Intercession pulls us into a very intimate relationship with God, allowing us to have a clearer understanding of God and get close to God's heart.

Summary

Intercessory prayer is a gift from God where the intercessor can stand in the gap on behalf of others and hear God's word on their behalf. Intercessors can be classified into four types: the general intercessor, the personal intercessor, the crisis intercessor, and the warfare intercessor.

Reflect and Respond

Is there a time when you have experienced the joy of serving as a specific intercessor? Are you sensitive to the nudging of God's Spirit to pray for another? Next time that nudging to pray for a person or a situation comes, heed it. Take time and let God guide your thinking. Pay attention if passages of Scripture seem to speak to you about God's purpose for that situation. Listen for God to give details that will help you pray more effectively. Though you may never know the whole situation, God is only asking you to be faithful. The results are God's. If, on some occasion you meet the person for whom you felt called to pray, let them know that they were laid on your heart and you prayed for them. If they want to give you information, listen quietly and thank God you were invited to pray on their behalf. Sometimes you may be given prophetic words to deliver to someone. Test those with the person to see if they understand what they mean.

---

[1] Cindy Jacobs, *Possessing the Gates of the Enemy* (Grand Rapids, MI: Chosen Books, 1991), p. 40.
[2] Wagner, Peter, *Prayer Shield* (Ventura, CA: Regal Books, 1992), p. 34.
Other Sources
   Cindy Jacobs, *The Voice of God* (Ventura, CA: Regal Books, 1995).
   Dutch Sheets, *Intercessory Prayer* (Ventura, CA: Regal Books, 1996).
   Peter Wagner, *Warfare Prayer* (Ventura, CA: Regal Books, 1992).

CHAPTER 7

Prayer and Fasting

During my third term in Kenya as a missionary nurse, God opened the way for me to start holding ten-week Bible studies in the villages. It was a challenge to weave those studies into the fabric of my extended hours at the hospital. I was happy when it was possible to turn my work at the hospital over to a qualified Kenyan nurse.

God also had graciously led a Kenyan friend to share in the leadership of the Bible studies. Sammy's astute understanding of his people and his ability to see the areas of his culture I didn't understand made this experience especially meaningful to me. Instead of people coming into my "turf" where I was at home, I was going into their turf and learning so much about their culture I could never have learned at the hospital. At the same time, I became acutely aware of the hunger in their lives for a much deeper understanding of God and the Bible and a desire to adapt those teachings into their lives.

I was faced with a difficult decision. Was my work finished in Kenya or was God calling me to focus some time in developing the Theological Education by Extension Program and preparing leadership to continue those village studies? I needed to think about my long-term future. I was in my late thirties and had been away from American nursing for the most of sixteen years. Financially I had been able to set aside very little, though I had learned that God keeps his promises and provides for our needs. Time and time again I experienced God's affirmation of his call to do village studies. There had been no budget for such an endeavor yet there were many expenses incurred. The cost of the study books for daily assignments for each student was prohibitive for many. To offset that, I arranged for them to pay half while I trusted I would find ways to subsidize the remaining costs. Transportation itself was a financial concern with gas prices holding around $3 a gallon. Never before had I experienced receiving undesignated checks in the mail to the extent that I did at that time. I could use them in this new ministry! However, there were times when there was no cash to buy the gas. I would say to Sammy as we would discuss the travel for the next day that I didn't have cash for the gas but we would plan to go. Without fail, someone would show up, sometimes late at night, with money they had borrowed from me at some other time. Since I had made it a conscious decision that I would not keep track of people who owed me money, I never knew if what was returned was the whole amount but what I did know was that it was the right amount for the gas.

Life was so hectic before I left Kenya that time. While I was unsettled about my return, God was busy bringing people into my life with similar concerns for developing strong spiritual leadership in the villages. I began to see a design forming. It became obvious that there needed to be some cultivation in the villages so people would be spiritually ready to benefit the most from these studies. God brought an evangelist who was concerned that though he witnessed people's lives being transformed by the power of God's love, he knew that many of them would not get the nurture in their churches that would help them grow in their faith. It also became clear to me that while the studies provided a foundation for church leadership, there needed to be further teaching specifically on the role of church leaders. At a surprise meeting, I discovered that a teacher at the Bible School held the same concern and was already spending some of his weekends going out in the villages and conducting classes with church leaders. What was God trying to say to us? Was God actually designing a team that could be used to raise the level of spirituality in the Kenya churches? The evangelist would go first, followed by the ten-week study, followed with special training for those in leadership roles. Was God trying to tell me that I was to lay aside my nursing profession and return to Kenya to work through Friends Bible Institute [now known as Friends Theological College]? I felt a great thud in my body when I considered this. What about my future?

With little time to reflect and process what God was saying to me, I returned to the States knowing that I needed time alone where I could fast and pray. I had never actually fasted before, and I knew very little about it. But I knew it was the only way for me to seek God's face and find clarity.

Although my family didn't understand my motive, I arranged to stay in a corncrib converted into a cabin beside a pond in the middle of a field. My plan was to spend three days, without interruption, fasting and praying. Those days proved to be very important as I came to understand that indeed, I was to give up my nursing profession at least for a time and return to Kenya to develop the Theological Education by Extension Program through Friends Bible Institute.

Fasting is something discussed many times in the Bible. Esther called people to fast and pray before she risked her life to talk with the king (Esther 4:16). Moses fasted and prayed forty days and forty nights at the time he was given the Ten Commandments (Deuteronomy 9:9). Daniel abstained from "choice food, meat and wine" for three weeks and experienced God's response to his setting "his mind to gain understanding" (Daniel 10:3-12). Jesus fasted for forty days and nights while he was being tempted (Luke 4:1-13). Paul did not eat or drink anything for three days immediately after his dramatic conversion (Acts 9:9). There are many other incidents mentioned in Scripture. To my knowledge, however, I don't see that there is a command to fast on a regular basis. Instead there should be a willingness to do so if God so urges.

Jesus and his disciples were criticized once for not fasting. At the time Jesus in essence told them that while the bridegroom was with them, they were feasting, but when the bridegroom was taken from them, they would fast (Matthew 9:15). I gather that Christ upheld the discipline of fasting and expected his followers to do it.

Yet fasting is not a common practice today. When fasting is mentioned, it is amazing how many people will respond negatively, saying it is unwise to treat our bodies in that way. We must have three meals a day. People assume that fasting will bring about weakness. According to Richard Foster, fasting developed a bad reputation during the Middle Ages. The inward reality of the Christian faith had declined to such an extent that what developed was only the outward form of faith in the discipline of fasting with its extremely rigid regulations. Modern culture reacted strongly to those excesses and for nearly one hundred years very little, if anything, was written about fasting. Apparently for the most part the practice has been disregarded.[1] When we look back at godly people who have done mighty things for God, it is interesting how many of them testify to the necessity of prayer with fasting. Today fasting is once again beginning to find a place in the lives of individuals and some churches, particularly as spiritual reawakening is anticipated.

Purpose of Fasting

When fasting is included with prayer, we experience more keenly the truths of God. If we are seeking guidance and direction for something specific, we find that clarity comes when fasting is combined with prayer. Fasting cannot be looked on as a ritual completed. Bill Bright says, "Fasting reduces the power of self so that the Holy Spirit can do a more intense work within us."[2] Richard Foster comments that fasting must forever center on God. It should be God initiated and God ordained. It is often through fasting that we are enabled to identify those things that control us. In dealing with those new insights, we are helped to be more like Jesus. Fasting is helpful in keeping a good balance in our lives. It is easy to become enslaved with things we crave without realizing that those nonessentials are taking priority in your life. Fasting allows us to see more clearly what is important. Fasting may increase the effectiveness of intercessory prayer, give guidance in decisions, increase concentration, and give deliverance from bondage.[3] The important thing is to keep focused on God and not focus on our bodies.

Is Fasting for Everyone?

Fasting is probably not for everyone. There are some people who should never fast without professional supervision. It is probably wise to consult a doctor before entering into the fast.

Deciding to Fast

Since there are no specific rules about fasting, we need to respond to our sense of call to fast. Should there come an inner urge to seek God in a special way or a desperate need or a compelling circumstance, it may be the Holy Spirit calling us into a special time of fasting. Experiencing the benefits of fasting will make it easier to determine when a fast is appropriate. Since the practice of fasting has been given less emphasis, it may be important to proclaim a fast and see what God teaches us in the process.

I once felt a concern to set aside one day a month for a fast. I learned very quickly that I needed to have a specific objective for fasting. Did I seek spiritual renewal or guidance, healing, resolution for some problem?

Bill Bright offers the following guide to prepare for a fast.[4]
1. The first question that needs to be addressed is "Why are you fasting?"
2. Prepare yourself spiritually before beginning a fast. Start by humbling yourself before God and repenting of

any known sins, for sin in your life can hinder your prayers (Psalm 66:16-20).
3. Prepare yourself physically by eating smaller meals for a few days prior to beginning the fast.
4. Seek God's leading for the kind of fast you are to undertake. How long will this fast be—twenty-four hours, three days, many days or weeks? Starting with a twenty-four-hour partial fast is a good way to begin your experience of fasting. Guidelines for maintaining a fast are given in Bill Bright's book, *The Coming Revival: America's Call to Fast, Pray, and 'Seek God's Face.'*
5. Plan your fast at times when you can limit your activity level but maintain your usual schedule as much as you can. Allow adequate times for rest. Remember that Jesus told the people that fasting should not be obvious to others (Matthew 6:16-18), therefore you need to maintain personal hygiene and go about activities as normally as possible.
6. If you are on prescribed medications, consult with your doctor the advisability of going on a fast prior to beginning the fast. Is it safe to continue taking the medication or should some adjustment be made?
7. The purpose of fasting is to grow into a closer relationship with God. That means we set aside ample time to be alone with the Lord to pray, to study the Word, to meditate and give attention to spiritual matters. Expect this to be a growing, insightful time with God. Follow through on what you are given.

Even while you continue your daily routines, keep as focused as possible on what is happening spiritually.
8. Bring your fast to an end with a light meal of fresh fruits and vegetables and gradually increase your intake.

Fasting can also be a powerful corporate experience. It will be discussed in chapter 10.

Summary

Fasting was a common practice in the Bible for both individuals and for groups of people. Though there doesn't seem to be a command for fasting, Jesus told the disciples when they asked why they were unable to drive out the evil spirit on one occasion that "This kind can come out only by prayer and fasting" (Mark 9:29).

The purpose of fasting is strictly to humble ourselves before God and open our heart to richer and deeper understanding of God and God's purposes. It is a time to seek direction and clarity. Suggestions for preparing for a fast are as follows:

1. Determine why you are fasting.
2. Prepare yourself spiritually for the fast by repenting of any sins.
3. Prepare yourself physically by cutting back on food intake two to three days prior to fasting.
4. Determine the kind of fast you will participate in— partial or full and determine the length of your fast.
5. Limit your activity and allow adequate time for rest.
6. Consult your physicians regarding any prescribed medication as you plan your fast.

7. Set aside time to pray, study the Word, meditate as God leads you into things of the spirit.
8. Bring the fast to an end with a light meal of fresh fruits and vegetables and gradually increase your intake.

REFLECT AND RESPOND

What is your attitude toward fasting? If you are facing a difficult decision or feel a yearning for gaining a closer relationship with God, set aside one day to fast and pray using some of these suggestions to get started.

---

1. Robert J. Foster, *Celebration of Discipline* (San Francisco, CA: Harper & Row, 1978), p. 41.
2. Bill Bright, *The Coming Revival: America's Call to Fast, Pray, and 'Seek God's Face,'* (Orlando, FL: NewLife Publications, Campus Crusade for Christ. 1995), p. 93. ©Bill Bright, 1995. All rights reserved. Used by permission.
3. Foster, Ibid., p. 48-49.
4. Bright, Ibid., pp. 128-142.

CHAPTER 8

Praying When God Seems Distant

Sometimes even though we pray, God seems silent. Often it is those times that we lash out and say that prayer doesn't do any good, or we blame God for not responding to our prayers. These responses must grieve God's Spirit, for God is a loving God who hears the prayers spoken honestly from our hearts. So why are there times when God seems silent and distant?

GOD'S SILENCE MAY MEAN THAT GOD WANTS TO REVEAL SOMETHING NEW TO US.

Mary and Martha probably asked that same question when their brother, Lazarus, lay sick. The sisters sent word to Jesus that their brother was ill. Yet Jesus didn't immediately hurry to their home in Bethany. The Scriptures assure us that Jesus very much loved this family. Why then did he wait to go when he knew he could heal Lazarus? Jesus showed up after Lazarus had died and after the family had gone through the rituals that surrounded death. Is it surprising that both Martha and Mary blame Jesus for their brother's death? Both of them said, "If you had been here, my brother would not have died"

(John 11:21, 32). No doubt they were disappointed that Jesus had failed them at a crucial time in their lives.

But look at what Jesus said. When he was first approached, Jesus said, "This sickness will not end in death. No, it is for God's glory so that God's Son may be glorified through it" (John 11:4). Later when the disciples tried to persuade him not to go because of imminent danger, Jesus told them that Lazarus was asleep. The disciples jumped on that and said that if Lazarus were sleeping, he would be all right. They didn't know that Jesus meant that Lazarus had died. But listen to Jesus' words as he explained that Lazarus was dead: "for your sake I am glad I was not there, so that you may believe" (John 11:15).

Why did Jesus delay his appearance in this home? Didn't the sisters have sufficient faith? Jesus knew they were ready to learn a greater truth about him. And what was it Jesus wanted to reveal to them? He wanted them to know that Jesus is the resurrection and the life. "The silence of God means that he is ready to bring into our lives a greater revelation of himself than we have ever known."[1]

THE ANSWER MAY BE DIFFERENT FROM WHAT WE EXPECTED.
Other times when we pray for something, it seems the answer that comes is different from that for which we prayed. During my first term as a missionary nurse in Kenya, I lived with a teacher in a house provided through the school. Housing was a major problem. Each institution at the mission was expected to provide housing for its staff. All the housing at the hospital was occupied. When another teacher came for

the Girls High School, it was reasonable that I should move so that teacher could have a place to live.

I prayed a lot about this situation but nothing seemed to come available. The new teacher moved in, leaving us quite crowded. I began to pray more earnestly. I remember saying to God that I really didn't believe he had called me to Kenya to live under a tree, so he needed to reveal to me what I was supposed to do. In the silences following that prayer, it seemed to me that God said, "I've always wanted to be your friend, Mary Glenn, but you've always turned to your other friends first."

Now that didn't solve my problem of housing, but it did bring me into a deeper and greater appreciation for God. God was my friend! God cared about my situation! I could trust him to help me solve this problem, but first I had to be stripped of my friends so God could reveal himself to me in such a dynamic way. Yes, housing did work out with a very caring family who welcomed me warmly and gave their friendship to me in loving ways, but also my relationship with God had grown dramatically as those details were worked out.

When answers come that are different than expected, we may fail to see that the things that are happening are part of the answer. We tend to call them distractions and fail to connect them with God's answer. We need to be alert to how those distractions are part of the answer and to see that God is at work in a different way than we prayed. When this happens, we need to adjust our lives and move with what God is doing.

GOD CAN BRING GOOD OUT OF DIFFICULT SITUATIONS.

It would be rare to ask God to bring unpleasant things into our lives. Our tendency is to ask God to make us well or keep us from suffering. On occasion, we may feel that God hasn't heard our prayer because we have had to endure suffering. Does that mean that God has not heard our prayer? 1 Peter 4:19 explains what is happening. "So then, those who suffer according to God's will should commit themselves to their faithful Creator and continue to do good." Often suffering is allowed, and God can bring something very good out of that suffering.

I have referred to the traumatic experience when I was assaulted. I prayed that God would stop that man from carrying out his intentions. Though that wasn't to be, I never felt rejected by God. God had a lot to teach me. Several months later, a lady came to visit me. When she was a child, her stepfather had molested her. There had never been reconciliation between the two of them.

It had been important for me to respond to the many people who had sent me cards and letters during my recovery. In one of those letters, I had updated my progress and the latest information on the search for my perpetrator. I had mentioned that I felt that justice should be done for the behavior exhibited, but that I hoped that my perpetrator would experience a relationship with Jesus and find meaning for life.

When this woman had received my letter, she realized that I had been able to forgive the man for what he had done to me. At that moment God had spoken to her and had told her that she needed to call her stepfather and tell him that she forgave him for what he had done. It was not an easy call to make, but she had done it—and over the phone he had given his heart to Jesus. Shortly after that, he had been diagnosed with lung cancer and within three months, he had died. At the funeral some of his family had seen such a remarkable change in his life in those three months that they too had wanted to follow Jesus.

Suffering can open the door for God to do a mighty work. Does it mean that God doesn't hear our prayers? Does it mean that God doesn't care about the things we are going through? Does it mean that God sends the suffering? I think not. I think it means that just because we are following Jesus does not exempt us from suffering. It has a lot to do with how we respond to the suffering. When we trust God to bring something good out of those situations, we are able to focus on how God is at work in those situations and spend less time worrying about ourselves.

BARRIERS CAN PREVENT OUR PRAYERS FROM BEING ANSWERED.

When we realize that the prayer as we prayed it seems not to be answered in our anticipated way, we may need to examine ourselves and see if there are barriers that are preventing our prayers from being answered.

Sin. Check to see if your relationship with God is intact. Jesus said, "Blessed are the pure in heart, for they will see God" (Matthew 5:8). In Isaiah 59:1-2 we read "...your iniquities [sin] have separated you from your God; your sins have hidden his face from you, so that he will not hear." In order for God to hear us, we need to make sure our relationship is right with God and that there is no sin raising a barrier between us. Unconfessed sin may be a barrier preventing God from hearing our prayers. Sometimes we go about our lives without recognizing that what we are doing is displeasing to God until it is somehow brought to our attention.

Many years ago when a Bible school student of mine was teaching Sunday school in one of the villages, she invited the children to bring their offerings. Some coins were placed at the front of the church as well as eggs, maize, pineapples, and live chickens. She noticed that there was mold on some of the corn and that some of the eggs were rotten. She talked with the children about how it must grieve God to see them bring gifts that were spoiled. How would the church be able to make those gifts useful in ministry? But even more, what did it say about the one giving those gifts—that they thought so little of God that they gave something of no use instead of giving with love and joy for what God had given them? It was a time for confession.

Unbelief. Another barrier is unbelief. In Matthew 21:22, we read "If you believe, you will receive whatever you ask for in prayer." How important to pray, believing that God will hear and answer our prayers.

Unforgiving spirit. Holding grudges or having an unforgiving spirit can be a hindrance to God's hearing our prayers. Jesus talked about this in Matthew 5:22-24. He said that if we hold a grudge or are angry with a brother or sister and come to the altar with a gift for the Lord, we must first be reconciled to our brother or sister and then come and offer our gift to God. Our attitudes for one another can affect our prayers.

One of the teachers at the mission Bible school had the unfortunate experience of getting a young woman pregnant out of wedlock. The community turned against that teacher in extreme ways. He felt very alone. I, too, was disappointed. As I wrestled with the situation, I became aware that God wanted me to visit the teacher. That seemed awkward. I felt it unwise to visit him alone, so I invited a young man who knew the situation to accompany me.

It was hard to know how to approach this situation. I could only trust that God would go before us. The teacher invited us in. He began to pour out his heart and talk about his feelings of remorse. We sat together and listened. When it seemed right, we began to talk about God's willingness to forgive if we confess our sins. We remembered David and his powerful prayer of confession in Psalm 51. I will never forget the heartfelt way this teacher read that prayer. When we were about ready to go, the teacher made the comment that we were the first ones willing to listen to him and to learn how truly sorry he was for his behavior. Though he was removed from his position at the Bible school, both of us had learned some very important lessons. He had learned the true meaning of God's forgiveness. I had learned that to hold a grudge can hinder my prayers.

Wrong motive. Another barrier is praying with the wrong motive. James 4:3 says, "When you ask, you do not receive, because you ask with wrong motives, that you may spend what you get on your pleasures." How easy it is to ask for something selfishly, and then if God doesn't give it to us, blame God for not hearing. Jesus lovingly told us how important it was that we keep connected to him. He said, "remain in me, and I will remain in you" (John 15:4), and again in John 15:5, Jesus said, "I am the vine; you are the branches. If anyone remains in me and I in them, they will bear much fruit; apart from me you can do nothing." In other words, when we keep connected with Jesus, we will know him intimately and can pray according to his will.

When my brother was young, he became very sick with strep throat. The antibiotics known today were not available. The doctor did all he knew to do but told my parents that he probably had a fifty-fifty chance of survival. They cared for him at home with the help of a live-in nurse. My Dad tells how he prayed and prayed that his son's life would be saved, yet there seemed to be no improvement. On about the tenth day, my Dad said that he found himself praying differently. He told God that he would like very much to raise this child but if God chose to take him, he would offer his son to God. It was that day that the fever broke and my brother began his slow, but steady, recovery. Dad shared that story because of the great lesson he had learned: that when we pray we have to want God's will to be done and not make demands that will give us satisfaction alone.

Jesus prayed for God to remove the cup of death on the cross from him, but God knew the larger picture. Jesus was able to pray "Yet not as I will, but as you will" (Matthew 26:39). We feel the impact of that prayer yet today.

God's answer sometimes is no. That is an answer. The importance of that answer may not be understood until later. Moses had to deal with God's no in answer to his request to cross the Jordan and see the Promised Land. Earlier Moses had become angry when the people he was leading had cried for water. In his frustration, Moses had beaten the rock instead of speaking to it as God had told him to do to call forth water. At that time, God had informed Moses that he could not be allowed to cross into the land of Canaan. But as they got closer, Moses must have yearned to see that land. God remained true to his earlier decision. Moses was a leader, and he had disobeyed God. The people needed to learn that disobeying God is followed with consequences.

In his book *When God Says No*, Leith Anderson reminds us that prayer is based on relationship—the better the relationship, the better the prayer. "It's when we know and love God for himself that we develop the intimacy that results in prayers heard and requests granted."[2]

Stop praying too soon. Sometimes we stop praying too soon. We grow impatient. What we don't realize is that sometimes many changes have to occur—in the lives of others, or in our own life—for the answer to come. Those changes may take time. God may want to give us more than we are asking for. An example of this is the story of Hannah. Hannah was unable to conceive a child. This was complicated by the fact that her husband's other wife taunted her, leaving her very sad. She prayed and prayed that God would give her a child. The Israelites at that time were not following God well. God was looking for a leader who would lead well. In 1 Samuel 1, we read how Hannah began to change her prayer. She told God that if God would give her a son she would give him back to the Lord. She was faithful, and when Samuel was born she took him to the temple where he later was recognized as a great leader of Israel. God knew when the time was right to answer this prayer. Hannah never stopped praying until the prayer was answered, while God was working out the changes in Hannah's life and preparing the necessary leader for the Israelite people.

In the Sermon on the Mount, Jesus said in Matthew 7:7, "Ask and it will be given to you; seek and you will find; knock and the door will be opened to you." Some translate this to keep on asking, keep on seeking, and keep on knocking, for then answers will come.

Summary

There are times when we feel that God is silent even though we are praying in the best manner we know. At times like that keep doing the last thing you felt God led you to do until new insights are given. Realize that God may be preparing to bring a greater revelation of himself. Look for that to come. God may answer your prayers differently than you expected. When seeming distractions follow your prayers, look to see what God is doing and change your direction in line with God's.

Though we prefer to live a life of comfort, sometimes we are allowed to suffer. How we respond in those difficult situations will help us be alert to the good that God may bring out of our suffering.

When we feel our prayers are going unanswered, check to see if there are barriers that keep God from hearing and answering our prayers. Possible barriers are sin, unbelief, an unforgiving spirit, a wrong motive, and stopping prayer too soon.[3]

Reflect and Respond

Are you experiencing God's silence now? Patiently consider if God wants to reveal something new to you and be open to that possibility. Is the answer turning out to be different than you expected? Can you accept a different answer? Is there a barrier between you and God, such as sin, an unforgiving spirit, or a wrong motive? Is it possible you have given up on God's response too soon? If you have been journaling your prayers, this is a good time to reread those prayers. You may find that there are answers that have come or that your motives were not right. Do your part to adjust your thinking and attitude so your relationship with God will be whole.

---

1 Henry Blackaby and Claude V. King, *Experiencing God* (Nashville, TN: Lifeway Press, 1990), p. 94.

2 Leith Anderson, *When God Says No* (Minneapolis, MN: Bethany, 1996), p. 83.

3 Grace and Fred Holland, *Talking With God* (Kisumu, Kenya: Evangel Publishing House, 1972), pp.76-91.

Other Resources

  Paul Cedar, *A Life of Prayer* (Nashville, TN: Word Publishing, 1998).

  Evelyn Christenson, *What Happens When Women Pray* (Colorado Springs, CO: Chariot Victor Publishing, 1975, 1991).

CHAPTER 9

My House Shall Be Called a House of Prayer

On Jesus' triumphal entry into Jerusalem, he went to the temple. At the sight of people buying and selling and moneychangers busy at work, Jesus overthrew their tables and reminded them of the purpose of the temple. It was not for personal gain. It was not for carrying on business. "My house will be called a house of prayer…," Jesus said, quoting from the words of Isaiah (56:7). It is a place for worshipping God.

As we look at the important place of corporate prayer, I want to be clear about the definition of corporate prayer. Corporate prayer occurs when a significant part of a local church gathers together with the intention to pray. It can expand to include many churches gathering together with the intention to pray for common concerns.

Our society strongly encourages individual rights. This thought pattern has subtly found its way into the church making it very difficult to experience fully the power of corporate leading for the body of Christ.

As I visit churches, I have found that prayer is considered something very private. Many people say they pray alone. Yet when opportunity is given to pray together, people fall silent, seemingly unable to talk with God when in the presence of others. The forces of evil are very afraid of prayer. Are our churches weak because we are not claiming the power of prayer?

The New Testament church provides a wonderful model for corporate prayer. In fact, the church was born out of corporate prayer. Before Jesus ascended, he told the disciples to wait in Jerusalem "until you have been clothed with power from on high" (Luke 24:49). In Acts 1 we read how the disciples went to the upper room and devoted themselves to prayer. Their prayers were dramatically answered by the coming of the Holy Spirit on the day of Pentecost. They were empowered to establish the early church. They recognized the power of prayer and made it a central part of their life together.

So how does corporate prayer strengthen the church? First, when people pray together, the strength of many prayers is greater than an individual prayer. Just as Ecclesiastes 4:12b reminds us: "A cord of three strands is not quickly broken." So it is when we pray together. Not only does God hear the petitions made but also the gathered people hear each other and the depth of prayer increases.

As we listen to one another pray, we hear each other's hearts. God is able to bring various perspectives together opening the way for unity and direction. It is a most moving experience.

A second aspect of corporate prayer is the power of agreement. Jesus says in Matthew 18:19 that "if two of you on earth agree about anything you ask for, it will be done for you by my Father in heaven." Again we understand that agreement in prayer is more effective when people are gathered in prayer rather than the solitary prayer of an individual.

A third aspect of corporate prayer is that the body of Christ shares the prayer experience and therefore observes together how God's power is demonstrated. Henry Blackaby, in his book *Experiencing God*, tells how the church he was pastoring experienced God's power through prayer when they wanted to be faithful in planning their church's budget. A member of the finance committee became concerned that the church needed to plan their budget on the basis of faith rather than on the anticipated income. His suggestion was that first they should determine all that God wanted to do through that church. Then they needed to determine what that would likely cost. Then they should base their income on what they could expect from tithes, what others promised to do, and what they would depend on God to provide.

The church prayed together about it and decided this was really the approach God wanted them to take in planning their budget. Their normal budget would have been around $74,000, but when they estimated the cost for what they believed God wanted to do through them that year, the budget came to $164,000. After some discussion, they accepted, by faith, that the operating budget would be the grand total and that they would credit God with any moneys that came in from unanticipated sources. They also agreed that they would daily pray for God to provide for their needs. When the year came to an end, they had received $172,000 toward their budget. They had prayed together. They had stepped out by faith together. They were able to see God's power demonstrated and rejoice together.[1]

When you think about the church as a House of Prayer, turn your thoughts to your own church. How do you feel about praying your church to its potential? Is your church a House of Prayer? Does corporate prayer take place regularly? Do you find unity in God's leading as a faith community?

Dian Ginter and Glen Martin, authors of *Power House*, have done a careful study of churches through which they have identified four kinds of churches in relation to prayer. They looked at the levels of will and skill to pray as they made their study. Study the following four descriptions of churches[2] and ask God to help you see which group most closely describes your church.

THE PROMISING CHURCH

People within the Promising Church have a low level of will to pray and little skill. It is expected that worship, Sunday school classes, and other meetings will open and close with prayer, like bookends. There is very little emphasis on prayer and virtually no teaching about prayer. If someone in the church makes the effort to invite people to prayer, he or she becomes frustrated as there is little response and results of those who do covenant to pray are lacking. The congregation has had little exposure to understanding the power of prayer. There is usually more indifference or frustration in prayer than actual resistance to it. Given some intentional visioning and modeling, this church could begin the journey toward becoming a House of Prayer.

The Progressing Church

The Progressing Church has a low will to pray but a medium amount of skills. They often are the churches that have been around for some time and in the past have had some significant prayer meetings. For some reason, interest has declined and those who do pray find themselves praying words over and over and experiencing boredom in their life of prayer. There is general apathy toward prayer. Perhaps their prayers have become so general that there is no way to identify God's answers. For example, if we pray "for all the missionaries around the world," what are we expecting to see God do? Prayer needs to be balanced with the acknowledgment of God's responses. That helps to bring trust that God is a hearing and answering God. If people have little involvement with the church, they will lack vision and purpose for praying, another factor that will lead to apathy toward corporate prayer.

Midweek prayer meetings have been an important part of many long-established churches. Yet the attendance has dwindled in many instances until they no longer meet as a faith community with the intention to pray. C. Peter Wagner suggests that there are good reasons why people choose not to attend. First, he says, is because the meetings are boring. Second, many people go only to be spectators. They have no contribution to make to the prayer time. Third, people claim that their personal needs are not met. This is a wrong concept, for meeting one's personal needs should not be the principal motivation for corporate prayer. Of course, if there are pressing personal needs, they can be made a matter of prayer as the corporate body. But corporate prayer should be focused more intently on the things that affect the whole body. Fourth, people admit they do not know how to pray in public, and they feel ill at ease. Fifth, people claim they don't see any evidence of God's Spirit being present. Sixth, there doesn't seem to be anything happening in response to prayer so why continue such a useless exercise? Seventh, sometimes the prayer meeting becomes only a time to gossip about things that really don't need to be shared with as much detail. Prayer should be sincere and genuine with enough information being shared only to help others pray more specifically.[3]

For Progressing Churches to move on to a more healthy prayer life, they need to allow the Spirit to help them recognize their present need. Members may have to review the church's history and realize where they have gone astray. Corporate repentance to correct these weaknesses will begin the process toward health.

THE PRODUCTIVE CHURCH

The Productive Church has both a wide range of praying skills and the will to pray. They just lack exposure to differing prayer styles. These churches will often have significant praying going on through small groups but widespread prayer practice is limited. Providing opportunities for people to experience different styles of praying together can help this church move toward becoming a Powerful Church.

THE POWERFUL CHURCH

It is the Powerful Church in which prayer is positioned, theoretically and practically, at the center of all the church does. Prayer is seen as being as important as evangelism, discipleship, and missions. Virtually every activity, meeting or church event will be undergirded with prayer. These churches also know the impact of God's blessings and power. They often see growth. They acknowledge God's blessings as their financial and spiritual needs are met. Prayer is important to the church leaders as well as to the body of Christ. Members are comfortable with a wide variety of prayer styles. Regular teaching on prayer for all ages is planned and carried out. Groups of people spontaneously pray together at the close of worship or other gatherings. Prayer seminars and conferences are very important. There is always room to develop the life of prayer within the church.

As you look at these four descriptions of churches and their relation to prayer, do you identify one as being descriptive of your meeting or church? Are you being called to lead your church to a more vital prayer life?

Summary

Corporate prayer occurs when a significant part of a local church gathers together with the intention to pray. It can expand to include many churches gathering together with the intention to pray for common concerns.

Corporate prayer begins when individuals within the body of Christ are committed to prayer and recognize the strength that comes when prayer is shared with more people. As people talk with God and hear each other pray, God is able to bring their perspectives together in the power of agreement. When the body of Christ shares in prayer, they have the opportunity to experience how God's power is demonstrated and can rejoice in that together.

Churches express different relationships to prayer. The *Promising Church* has a low level of will to pray and little skill. To move on, the church will need some intentional visioning and modeling of prayer. The *Progressing Church* has a low will to pray but a medium amount of skill. This church can progress in its prayer life when members allow the Spirit to help them see where they have gone astray, repent, and begin to both model and teach others how to pray. The *Productive Church* has both a wide range of praying skills and the will to pray but not a lot of exposure to differing prayer styles. Offering opportunities for experiencing more variety in prayer will help these churches move toward becoming a House of Prayer. The *Powerful Church* is one in which prayer is positioned, theoretically and practically, at the center of all the church does. It is seen as being as important as evangelism, discipleship, and missions. There will always be more that God will have to teach the body of Christ about prayer.

RESPOND AND REFLECT

Take time to consider the place of corporate prayer in your church. How do you feel about praying your church to its potential? Do you find unity in God's leading as a faith community? Is God nudging you to begin a prayer ministry in your church? How will you respond?

---

[1] Henry Blackaby and Claude V. King, *Experiencing God* (Nashville, TN: Lifeway Press, 1990), p. 108.

[2] Glen Martin and Dian Ginter, *Power House* (Nashville, TN: Broadman & Holman Publishers, 1994), pp. 55-95. Used by permission.

[3] Peter C. Wagner, *Churches That Pray* (Ventura, CA: Regal Books, 1993), pp. 116-118.

CHAPTER 10

Dimensions of a Praying Church

*Y*ou may feel that prayer is certainly a part of your church. But does prayer saturate every aspect of your church life? If it did, how would it be different from what is already happening in your church? Consider what a House of Prayer, a place saturated with prayer, could look like.

The ten elements of a Praying Church mentioned here serve as a springboard for God to show you how your church or meeting can become a House of Prayer.[1]

1. PRAYER IS VISIBLE THROUGHOUT THE WORSHIP SERVICE.

When we gather for worship, we acknowledge the One we are worshipping through praise and prayer. A visitor coming for the first time should be able to know, without doubt, what the purpose of worship is and in whose name you are gathered.

Prayer should be visible from the pulpit. It is very important that the pastor, or a person within the gathered group, pray aloud on behalf of the congregation. Mention can be made of answers to prayer that have come during the past week. Through prayer, vision can be lifted to God as you corporately seek to fulfill what God is calling you to do. There may be some difficult decisions to be made together. There may be people within the congregation who are ill who can be remembered in prayer sometime during the service. For those who meet for worship without a pastor, be sensitive to God's yearning to hear someone lead your worship group in a conversation with God. Talking with God helps the gathered group know God's Presence is among you as you worship.

Often times, the one sharing the message can help the congregation appreciate the importance of prayer by talking about the vital place of prayer in Jesus' life or including other biblical characters for whom prayer changed the course of events.

It is not uncommon in Praying Churches to find people clustering in small groups to visit with one another before or following worship. Before their conversation ends, you will likely see them bow their heads and pray for one another before going their own ways.

2. Leadership is Committed to Prayer.

In a House of Prayer, the leadership is recognized as people who spend significant time with God in prayer each day. They will often model the importance of prayer as they go about their leadership roles within the faith community.

Perhaps the modeling I saw during my junior high years helped me believe in the power of prayer. My father accepted a pastorate in a small community in Iowa. It was quite an adjustment for our family when we moved. The house was much smaller. There were no cabinets or running water in the kitchen. There was no bathtub or shower, and the cook stove we were expected to use was an old wood burning stove. There were five of us, and only one walk-in closet. We had left a two-story home with plenty of room. However, it was clear that God had been in control of this change, and we were going to make the best of it.

The church building needed much attention. The people had decided earlier that year that because of lack of funds, they would only make necessary improvements on their church building rather than doing the needed major remodeling such as putting in indoor facilities, adding a kitchen and more classrooms. Then a tornado struck the church, lifting the belfry up and dropping it back into the church. The people saw God's hand in this and confessed that they had been willing to trust only in their resources and not to trust God to help them accomplish the important updating their building needed. They committed themselves to rebuilding the church, doing as much of the work as they could and trusting God for the necessary resources.

They held prayer meeting in the middle of the week faithfully. It was often during this time that I would hear the hearts of the people as they laid before God their needs for being obedient in providing the house for worship they believed God had led them to build. One of the leaders also had the most skill in carpentry and construction. He gave a tremendous amount of time at the church. One particular night, he prayed a prayer I will always remember. He said, "God, right now what we need is ready cash." We were at a place we could do no more work until we had money in hand. Within a week, the church received a check from someone living in Kansas who knew we were in the process of building a church. They said that if we could use it for flooring they would be happy, but if we needed it for something more urgent, we could use it for that. Flooring was exactly what we needed at that time. Because of that check, we were able to buy and lay the flooring so the building process could continue. A Praying Church will have leadership who demonstrate their commitment to prayer.

3. Prayer is included in all agendas.

Making prayer a part of all agendas from the most important gatherings to the least committee meeting makes a tremendous difference in the life of the church or meeting. These are not bookend prayers for opening and closing the meetings. These are intentional times of praying for concerns that arise. For example, during the Sunday school class time, it may become known that someone in the class is in need of prayer. Allow time to take that need to God in prayer before going on. Or if there are decisions to be made, allowing time to pray together about that concern will bring a quicker and more united understanding of what that decision should be. Learn to seek God's leading first rather than trying so hard on your own to find a solution and then admitting that you don't know what else to do except pray. Be careful that you don't spend a lot of time making plans and strategizing and then asking God to bless those plans. Include God as you address the issues.

4. Prayer is a part of the Christian education program.

Provide intentional teachings on prayer at all age levels. It is very important that children learn how to pray. Adults need the opportunity to expand their understanding of prayer. Some may have come into the fellowship only as adults and have not had the training as children. There is always more God wants to teach us about prayer.

Here are some examples for teaching or demonstrating prayer in Sunday school or small groups. Experience focusing your prayers on a specific concern; for example, pray for someone within the class who may be facing a difficult situation. The leader may need to give some guidance to keep the focus because people are so used to including many things in their prayers. Try using conversational prayer. (See chapter 11.) When the lesson has brought the class to the place where they are challenged to put what they have learned into action, introduce prayer to help the class understand how to seek God's leading to carry out their new learning appropriately. Take time to teach some praying skills to those who are new at praying. Some of the personal prayer styles we have discussed could be transferred to a group setting. For example, taking time to write out prayers using ACTS (see chapter 2) as a model can be a good experience.

Learning to sit in silence in a prayerful attitude is important. To begin, the leader may want to suggest that they enter a time of silence and meditation focusing on the concern at hand and asking God to show them the next step. Encourage the class to share the insights they receive from God. This can be powerful for often one will receive part of the whole picture while others will provide the remaining parts.

Introduce your class to praying in groups of twos and threes. For example, there may be specific concerns that the group is facing. Suggest that each of the groups choose to approach that concern from one of the following as they pray: Rejoice, Repent, Restore, Envision.

Review your curriculum and see if there are intentional times when students will learn or expand their experience with prayer. Provide times where your faith community is exposed to a variety of prayer styles. We will look at some of the corporate ways in following chapters.

5. Pastors and Key Leaders Are Given Strong Prayer Support.

Pastors and key leaders are easy targets for the evil one because wherever they go they represent the church. Yet they are human. They face temptations just like everyone else. They have feelings of inadequacy. They are often under stress usually brought on by unreasonable expectations of the congregation they serve. They yearn for a greater understanding of God so they can be used more effectively. Yet sometimes, a congregation would rather sacrifice their pastor than deal with the difficult situations that arise within the body. It is very important that prayers on behalf of the pastors and key leaders be in greater depth than simply asking God to bless them.

Colossians 1:9-12 can offer some language to give depth to our prayers. Notice the things in this passage for which we can pray will be given to our leaders. Paul prayed that the leaders would be filled with the knowledge of God's will, that they would be given spiritual wisdom and understanding, that they would lead lives worthy of the Lord, that they would bear fruit and grow in the knowledge of God. He also prayed that they would be given strength that comes from God's glorious power. He asked that they would be prepared to endure everything with patience and joyfully give thanks to God. Praying for the pastor and key leaders is vital to a Praying Church.

6. THERE IS A STRONG, CONSISTENT UNDER-GIRDING OF PRAYER FOR THE BODY OF CHRIST.

In addition to praying for the leadership, a Praying Church will have a strong, consistent under-girding of prayer for the members and attenders. Individuals will devote much of their time regularly praying for their church. These will not be "God bless our church, Amen" types of prayers. They will go much deeper.

Jesus gives a wonderful model for praying for the body of Christ in his prayer found in John 17:9-24. As you read this passage, note the highlighted things that Jesus prayed for his disciples and for the church.[2]

> 9 "I am asking on their behalf; I am not asking on behalf of the world, but on behalf of those whom you gave me, because they are yours. 10 All mine are yours, and yours are mine; and I have been glorified in them. 11 And now I am no longer in the world, but they are in the world, and I am coming to you. Holy Father, **protect them in your name** that you have given me, so **that they may be one, as we are one.** 12 While I was with them I protected them in your name that you have given me. I guarded them, and not one of

them was lost except the one destined to be lost, so that the scripture might be fulfilled. 13 But now I am coming to you, and I speak these things in the world so **that they may have my joy** made complete in themselves. 14 I have **given them your word**, and the world has hated them because they do not belong to the world, just as I do not belong to the world. 15 I am not asking you to take them out of the world, but I ask you **to protect them from the evil one.** 16 They do not belong to the world, just as I do not belong to the world. 17 **Sanctify them in the truth**; your word is truth. 18 As you have sent me into the world, so I have **sent them into the world**. 19 And for their sakes I sanctify myself, so that they also may **be sanctified in truth.**

20 "I ask not only on behalf of these, but also on behalf of those **who will believe in me through their word,** 21 that they may all be one. As you, Father, are in me and I am in you, may they also be in us, so **that the world may believe** that you sent me. 22 The **glory that you have given** me I have given them, so that they may be one, as we are one, 23 I in them and you in me, that they may become completely one, so **that the world may know that you have sent me and have loved** them even as you have loved me. 24 Father, I desire that those also, whom you have given me, **may be with me where I am, to see my glory**, which you have given me because you loved me before the foundation of the world" (John 17:9-24, NRSV).

When I pray with this prayer, I can almost feel Christ's compassion for me and for his bride, the church. Expect God to open a greater understanding of how to pray for the church as you use this model prayer.

7. Intercession is an integral part of the church life.

In a House of Prayer, there will be many ways in which prayer can be made on behalf of others within the church. There will be many opportunities for people to pray for situations within the church and those prayers will extend into the community, state, government, and world. Prayer chains may be established for those emergency situations when people need to be called to pray for those tough times. Small groups may gather regularly. A prayer room may be set aside within the church where individuals can come offer prayer on behalf of others and their needs. This is much more than a time of inward looking. This becomes a dynamic, powerful, and tangible way of having an impact both within the faith community and outside in the community.

8. Discernment of God's will for the church becomes evident.

Christians should be known for their love. Unfortunately in the church today, too often conflict runs rife. We have let the secular world influence the church in many ways instead of standing apart. Our society has become very individualistic. We think that we each have our own rights and when decisions have to be made, we demand our rights rather than considering what is best for the whole body or where God is leading us corporately.

In a House of Prayer, much prayer will be offered for the various facets of the church such as the education program, the outreach program, stewardship, peace and social concerns, the elderly and nursery, and the worship experiences. When business meetings come or decisions have to be made, people may already have been in conversation with God. It is possible they will come to the session with a sense of what the will of God is for that particular decision. Yet as people share their leadings, they listen carefully to one another while keeping the heart open for God's prompting. Many times what they will experience is that each person has contributed a piece in the whole puzzle and the direction that comes forward is clearly much better than what one person contributed. Often those decisions will carry the group into uncharted territory. Their faith may be challenged but if they are committed to adjusting their lives to doing what God is saying, they will discover their church is progressing and making a big difference in their community.

Sometimes congregations face difficult situations or extensive problems where there is need for seeking direction corporately. Fasting and praying together may be very powerful. Or when there are national or global crises, congregations or groups of congregations may find it beneficial to fast and pray together. Dr. Julio C. Ruibal provides the following for leading the congregation into a fast.[3]

Prepare the congregation by explaining the spiritual benefits and discussing the place of fasting in the Scripture. Make sure the congregation knows the specific reason a fast is called whether it is a specific need within the church, city, nation, or world.

Set a specific time for the corporate fast. Will it be one day, three days, or longer? It is suggested that it start on Sunday and that regular meetings be scheduled during the time when people can gather for corporate times of intercession.

Provide clear instructions for the fast. Provide people with adequate information for beginning the fast, for what to do during the fast, and how to break the fast.

Focus on prayer. When people are gathered together, allow time at the beginning for general worship but then break into small groups of four or six for an extended time of prayer.

Prepare for questions people may have as they go through the fast by setting up a "hotline" at which people may call and find someone with experience available to answer. Do not expect everyone to attend every day. Encourage everyone to fast and pray during the time the fast is called for but know that it will not be possible for everyone to attend every called gathering for prayer.

Teach the people to expect results and to watch to see what God is doing around them and within them. If specific guidance comes for follow-up, be prepared to do so.

9. Intentional plans for developing the prayer life of the congregation will be made.

When a church or meeting becomes intentional about developing a strong prayer life, they may decide that they need a Prayer Coordinator. This person will keep alive the emphasis on prayer, plan for intentional prayer teachings for all ages, introduce a variety of prayer styles for both individuals and the corporate group. For some large churches, they may find that this needs to be a paid staff person while smaller congregations may have a person within their fellowship who is willing to accept this role as a volunteer.

10. Prayer is extended into the community.

A Praying Church will soon realize that they cannot contain their prayers within the church. They will find ways to be more present in the community just as Jesus demonstrated. In chapter 13, suggestions will be made on how to pray in the community.

Glen Martin and Dian Ginter in their book *Power House* offer some practical plans to help a congregation and its leadership move into a more powerful corporate prayer ministry.

Summary

A House of Prayer will make prayer central to its ministry. Elements found in a Praying Church include the following:
1. Prayer is visible throughout the worship service.
2. Leadership is committed to prayer.
3. Prayer is included in all agendas.
4. Prayer is a part of the Christian education program.
5. Pastor and key leaders are given strong prayer support.
6. There is strong, consistent under- girding of prayer for the church.
7. Intercession is an integral part of the church life.
8. Discernment of God's will for the church becomes evident.
9. Intentional plans for developing the prayer life of the church will be made.
10. Prayer is extended into the community.

Reflect and Respond

Which of the dimensions of a praying church are you experiencing in your church? Are there one or two of these that particularly touch you and put within you a desire for your meeting to experience more fully? Listen for God to show you where to begin to see your faith community become a House of Prayer.

---

1 Glen Martin & Dian Ginter, *Power House* (Nashville, TN: Broadman & Holman Publishers, 1994), pp. 19-24. Used by permission.
2 John Maxwell, *Partners in Prayer* (Nashville, TN: Thomas Nelson Publishers, 1996), pp. 95-102.
3 Bill Bright, *The Coming Revival: America's Call to Fast, Pray, and 'Seek God's Face'* (Orlando, FL: New Life Publications, 1995), pp. 173-176. © 1995 Bill Bright. Used by permission.

CHAPTER 11

Learning to Pray as a Group

Amazing things happen to us when we share in prayer together. One of the joys of working with the nursing students in Kenya was our Friday evening Bible study. Some nursing students could not attend this fellowship because of work schedules, but usually there would be a good number of the students who came each week. In planning for these evenings, I decided to take a month to experience prayer. To help the students grow in their prayer life through learning to pray together, I introduced the concept of conversational prayer.

Conversational prayer is talking with one another as we talk with God. It happens in a similar manner to the way we converse in a group. One person contributes while others listen and someone responds or expands on what has already been said. And the conversation continues. The exciting thing is that the group directed its conversation to God.

After acknowledging Jesus' presence in our circle, thanking Jesus for each other and other things that came from our hearts, there was an amazing outpouring of love that could only have come from God. The expression of that love was poured on one another as we prayed and listened. The students had tasted the reality of God's presence. They didn't want to leave. The experience was so alive and vital that those who were present talked about it with others. The next three weeks nearly everyone not working became a part of this rich prayer time.

Thomas Merton writes, "Prayer is responding to God who loves you."[1] Somehow as we open ourselves to God and hear the hearts of others, our hearts become tender and we come to understand one another in deeper ways. Roselind Rinker describes conversational prayer as "a dialogue engaged in by people who are moving in love toward one another.... It is a conversation directed to God with us and within us, as well as to each other."[2] She continues her description of conversational prayer by saying that there are three ingredients common to any meaningful communication: becoming aware of the other and listening for what he/she is saying, meaning, or feeling; taking turns, listening, speaking, agreeing, and giving thanks; and keeping in tune so that there is full participation in the current subject until you are ready to move on.[3]

There is something very spontaneous about conversational prayer. It flows naturally through four main steps. In the beginning it is helpful to have someone give some guidance but as people become familiar with this method of praying together, it will flow as any conversation goes.

The four steps are as follows: God is present with us; Thank you, God; Help us, Lord; Help our friends/family. Use these steps to introduce praying together.

God is present. There is something special about inviting the group to stand together and to form a circle of love by holding hands (if this is uncomfortable, sit together in a circle).

A circle seems to symbolize our invisible union with Christ. Enter into a time of silent worship. Invite the group to find the attitude of prayer that is comfortable to them which may be closing their eyes to prevent being distracted by activity or focusing on an object that can move them into that place of worship and prayer.

Suggest that they silently release to God whatever is weighing on their minds or the plans they may be making. After pausing for people to do that, out of the silence, read these words of Jesus from Matthew 18:20: "For where two or three come together in my name, there am I with them." Give time for people to consider those words and then acknowledge that God is here. As you ponder that truth, suggest that the group imagine what it would be like if they were holding Jesus' hand in this circle. Would they feel the scars in his hand and remember the great sacrifice he made for them? When they lift their eyes to Jesus, do they see compassion and love as he tenderly looks at them? In acknowledging his presence, how would they describe their relationship with Jesus? Invite them to quietly worship Jesus.

After a brief silence, mention these expressions of Jesus. "My friend, I love you." "My friend, I accept you." "My friend, I care about you." "My friend, I forgive you...because, you see, I love you." Allow pauses between each phrase.

When the time seems right, pray a short prayer or pray: "Lord Jesus, we give you thanks for being with us, accepting us, loving each of us just as we are. We worship you now and forever."

After a moment of silence, stop and have the group sit down and talk about their experience as they acknowledged being in the presence of Jesus. What did they find helpful as they entered into prayer like this? What was significant for them as they imagined Jesus standing in the circle with them? Any time people enter into prayer whether alone or in a group, pausing to acknowledge Jesus' presence sets the stage for the prayer to happen meaningfully.

Thank you, God. Perhaps as you acknowledged God's presence, you found you really wanted to worship God by expressing praise and thanksgiving to God. That is a very natural response that will lead you into a deeper fellowship with God.

Some people feel self-conscious when they pray aloud. Others easily share their hearts with God. Take a short time to let people talk about their comfort or discomfort of praying audibly. Then invite the group to stand again and form a circle of love (or remain seated and hold one another's hands). Let them know that you will give guidance as you move into giving God thanks.

Make sure everyone knows the name of the person on his/her right and left. Then explain that the group will go around the circle asking each person to look at the person on his/her right and say, "Thank you, God, for _____;" then turn to the person on the left and say, "Thank you, God, for _____." Pause. Then the next person in the circle does the same thing to the two people on either side of him or her. Looking into the eyes of the other is powerful. If people in the group know each other and wish to give thanks for special things they know about one another, this is a good time to do that.

Give time to go around the circle. If the group is large, you may want to break into smaller groups of ten to twelve each. Continue by telling the group not to try to think of something to say, but if words come to them or their hearts start pounding or their hands get sweaty, God may be leading them to pray.

Encourage them to give their full attention to God and to open their hearts to Jesus. It is the time for giving thanks to God. The leader can often begin by saying something like, "Thank you, Jesus, for loving me." God is blessed when he hears prayers of thanks. One sentence is adequate. If someone wants to give thanks for another person, suggest they use only the first name. If someone in the group says the same thing someone else in the group was about to say, encourage the person to say it again. It is all right to be repetitive.

Don't rush this experience. Silent moments allow time for people to ponder the prayer already spoken and to listen if God should have a word for the others. In the beginning it also allows time for people to find courage to begin. When you sense it is time to move on, close with a prayer such as, "Thank you, Jesus, for all these prayers, and for the ones still in our hearts. Amen."

When people are learning to pray in this manner, take time to discuss the experience of thanking God. Was it an important time? What was most meaningful? This can be a very tender moment for the group as they hear one another giving God thanks for them. It is God's love flowing within the group. Acknowledging God's presence and giving thanks to God helps focus your conversation together.

Help me, Lord. Invite the group to sit in a circle as they move into asking God to help them. This is a time to experience the power of confession. The necessary courage to be honest in a group is found in God's acceptance and in each other's acceptance. Read from 1 John 1:9: "If we confess our sins, he is faithful and just and will forgive us our sins and purify us from all unrighteousness." Pause. Then read James 5:13-16: "Is any one of you in trouble? He should pray. Is anyone happy? Let him sing songs of praise. Is any one of you sick? He should call the elders of the church to pray over him and anoint him with oil in the name of the Lord. And the prayer offered in faith will make the sick person well; the Lord will raise him up. If he has sinned, he will be forgiven. Therefore confess your sins to each other and pray for each other so that you may be healed. The prayer of a righteous man is powerful and effective."

Knowing that God's love and acceptance is available to everyone, enter into an attitude of prayer. Invite the group to bring their personal needs, failures, and questions silently to Jesus and talk with Jesus about those areas of life where they feel inadequate or weak.

Allow several moments for people to pray quietly. Then lead in prayer or use a prayer like this one, "Thank you, Jesus, for hearing each one of us as we pray. Thank you for forgiving us the things we have confessed and for helping us to be honest in acknowledging our areas of needs." Invite the group to pray together these words as a closing to your prayer, "Thank you, Jesus."

Provide time now for people to express their needs verbally as they feel led. When one person is praying, encourage the others to lift that person to God in their hearts. If they want to add to that prayer, it is a wonderful way to realize that truly you are praying together. For example, the leader can help people by following someone's prayer by praying, "Hear Jessica's prayer, dear God, and grant her peace." That is a powerful way to affirm another.

Don't rush but when it seems right to bring this section to a close, simply say, "Amen." Focusing in prayer for ourselves gives us a place to leave our cares and concerns in God's hands so our hearts can be clear to pray for others. When praying in this manner for the first time, it is important to stop and discuss what people are experiencing.

Help our friends and family. To pray on behalf of another is to intercede for them. (See chapter 6.) It truly is an act of love. The Bible gives us guidelines to help us pray. From Matthew 7:7-11, Jesus taught that if we ask, we should receive. James reminded us that we need to pray according to God's will and not our own desires (James 4:2-3). Lead the group into an attitude of prayer.

Ask them to find that quiet place in their hearts and to seek the "mind of God" for the person they want to pray for. Though we cannot be the judge or the arbiter of another's fate, nor can we confess another's sins, we can join that person in praying to God on their behalf even if they are not present.

Begin with a prayer of love. Invite the group to name the person for whom they wish to pray in the quietness of their hearts and to give that person their love. Ask God to pour out his love on that person. Then hold the person in love. Some people may want to say the name aloud as the group waits expectantly in prayer.

Follow with a prayer of blessing for the person on your heart. Call on God's love and wisdom to give your person what he/she needs. Be careful not to impose your idea of what is best for this person. Here is a suggestion for praying a prayer of blessing, "Dear God, give to _____ the things that You in Your wisdom and love see that he/she needs."

Continue with the prayer of asking. Read Matthew 7:7,8: Ask and it will be given to you; seek and you will find; knock and the door will be opened to you. For everyone who asks receives and he who seeks finds, and to him who knocks it will be opened." People should be ready now to be specific as they pray for that which they believe God can do. There is a tendency at this point to want to tell the group their prayer concern. However, remind them that God is a part of the conversation so they need to tell everybody at the same time. In prayer then address the problem. Make faith-sized requests, meaning that you cannot make the answer come by your own power but you acknowledge God can bring it. Ask God boldly in a positive way. Let people respond to each other's prayers and add to them if they are led. When it seems timely to move to the next person's concerns, continue the prayers for others.

When the flow of conversation slows down and there is a sense that the group is finished, close with a prayer of praise to God for the opportunity to talk with God and for his listening to the prayers of each person's heart. Ask God to continue to teach you about prayer and to dismiss the group with God's peace and blessing. Allow time for people to share what they experienced as they entered into conversational prayer. Was it a good way to pray together?

Many times in Kenya when we would be facing another crisis at the hospital, I would find myself going to the home of one of the doctors. We would sit at the table, hold each other's hands and begin to pray in conversational prayer. We would begin with acknowledging that God was present with us and in our situation. It seemed like that would naturally make us give thanks for the answers to prayer we had already experienced or to give thanks for other things that we were grateful for. Thanks would quickly turn toward acknowledging our personal needs, and then we found ourselves praying for the concern that had brought us together. Those were very important moments. It didn't need to take long, but it helped us listen to God and discover direction that we probably would not have thought of on our own.

Conversational prayer helps us gain ease in talking with God aloud. It can be done as a family, within a prayer group, or during worship. It provides the opportunity to hear others praying which expands and strengthens the prayers already spoken or in the hearts of others.

Summary

Though conversational prayer is not a new style of praying together, it helps people gain confidence in praying aloud. It is a dialogue engaged in by people who are moving in love toward one another. The conversation is directed to God but involves the group.

Conversational prayer needs to flow naturally just as conversation flows when people are together in the same room. It provides a wonderful way for people who struggle to pray audibly to realize that praying is not scary but a loving thing to do together. Taking time to stop and talk about the segment of prayer you have experienced can be revealing and inspiring. However, as people become more familiar with this style of prayer, the conversation can flow. Acknowledging that Jesus is present leads to prayers of thanksgiving, which flows into prayers for oneself and then prayer for others. Taking time to hold the other in a prayer of love, followed with a prayer of blessing, prepares you to ask God for the specific concern.

REFLECT AND RESPOND

Gather as a family or your small group and experiment with conversational prayer. Take time to talk about the experience. The first time may seem a little stilted but as you become more familiar with this style of corporate prayer, you will find it comes naturally and expands your prayer experience.

---

1 Roselind Rinker, *Learning Conversational Prayer* (Collegeville, MN: The Liturgical Press, 1992), p. 13.
2 Roselind Rinker, *Teaching Conversational Prayer* (Waco, TX: Word Books, 1970), p. 22.
3 Ibid., p. 22.

Other Resource

Anne Thomas and Mary Glenn Hadley, editors, *Preparing Hearts and Minds* (Richmond, IN: Friends United Press, 1998), p. 13.

CHAPTER 12

Power in Corporate Prayer

When God wants to do something new among us, God calls people to pray. In the past 250 years, whenever a new spiritual awakening came, God's calling people to pray preceded it. Over the last decade or more, that calling again is occurring throughout our world. David Bryant of Concerts of Prayer International says that God is calling people to pray today in unprecedented ways—numerically, internationally, and across generations, denominations, ethnic groups, and walks of life. People in cities are gathering in city-wide prayer meetings for spiritual reawakening and wisdom in overcoming the social problems that afflict many of our communities. National prayer gatherings have been called. These prayer events are based on 2 Chronicles 7:14: "…if my people, who are called by my name, will humble themselves and pray and seek my face and turn from their wicked ways, then will I hear from heaven and will forgive their sin and will heal their land." People are joining together in praise marches to bring the whole body of Christ to agreement in public praise to God. Others are feeling called to journey into areas where the Gospel has not been clearly presented to pray on site with insight.

The media seldom picks up on these prayer efforts that seek to share God's love and concern for the world. For example, few people realize that specific people felt compelled to go to the Berlin wall and pray for that wall to come down. There are probably many others who had been praying for that to happen as well. In October 1989 the world was happy when the wall came down, in part because of these faithful people of prayer. Few people realize that the Soviet Church in 1987 called upon Christians around the world to pray for unity in their country as they faced many problems. We know now that the unwritten request was for deliverance from seventy years of captivity within the Bolshevik revolution. One hundred prayer networks responded to that request making January 1987 a special month of prayer for the Soviet Union. On the first working day of February of that same year, the then President Gorbachev released all religious prisoners. Their release began the chain of events that led to the ultimate breakdown of communism and an open door to the Gospel in most of Eastern Europe and Russia. Not everything has been smooth sailing since then in the Soviet Union. When God's power is evident in strong ways, the evil one raises up resistances, and we get caught in the midst of spiritual warfare. Our need for continued corporate prayer becomes more real as we seek God's guidance for the next steps.

In my own life I have experienced God's responding to the prayers of faithful people. A few years ago, a friend and I were asked to spend three-and-one-half months in Kenya at Friends Theological College. It was a critical time for the school as they were beginning the transition process of upgrading from a certificate standard to a diploma program. It seemed that every day, my friend and I met some crisis. Sometimes the electricity was shut off and we had to take the public transport to a nearby town, walk the streets to the electrical company, and wait our turn to discuss the reason for cutting off the electricity. Or a representative from the hospital would threaten to sue the school for noncompliance in paying bills that we may or may not have known about. Sometimes there was insufficient money to pay salaries on time. It was hard to get on with the task for which we had been sent.

One day some students informed me that they wanted to start a weekly prayer time and invited me to provide leadership for the first one. I was pleased that they were taking the initiative and gladly accepted the opportunity. I chose a style of corporate prayer that focused on God's vision for their school. It was a powerful time of sharing in prayer. As the weeks went on, this prayer group learned to pray conversationally, to put on the armor of God, to prayer walk through their village, and to find other ways to pray together.

But the difficult situations seemed to be outnumbering the positive. In my frustration one evening, I simply asked God to show me if anything spiritual was happening as a result of our being in Kenya. Within twenty-four hours, two students, at different times and places, came up to me with very similar comments. They said that this school term had been so different from other terms. Of course, I had to ask why. Without hesitation the response was, "It's the prayer life!" I can only thank God for that and trust that the prayer life continues to be strong and vital.

Throughout this book, we have looked at ways in which our personal prayer experience can mature. Developing our prayer lives helps corporate faith bodies to mature in their life of prayer as well. I am concerned that many of our churches find gathered prayer times uncomfortable. Is it because individuals are immature in their own prayer lives? Is it a tool of the evil one to prevent the church from experiencing God at a deeper level? Do we focus more on how prayer is made than on the Christ to whom we pray? Have we been so critical of one another that we have taken away the passion for corporate prayer? Does our discomfort indicate our level of faith? Or are we faced with apathy in our faith that prevents us from experiencing the richer life of prayer that God so longs for us to have?

Earlier in this book I referred to the uplifting experience I had while attending a conference in Chicago with people whom I didn't know. The first thing we did was spend two hours in corporate prayer. My reaction was one of awe. I felt united with people who cared about the same things I did. I was no longer a stranger as I heard the hearts of these people through their prayers. In fact, I felt as if I knew them better than many people I have been acquainted with for many years but who are very private in what God is allowed to do within their lives.

People often refrain from spending time praying together because they claim they don't see any results. That is probably more a statement of their belief system than the fact that God doesn't hear. Prayer can become alive and refreshing as we join together to pray for common concerns and renewal.

We may have to move out of our comfort zones and venture into some different styles of prayer.

Guided prayer often provides an opportunity for people to experience freshness in corporate worship. My experience with this has awakened something new in me. Guided prayer has become a time of celebration as the group enters into praise through song and prayers. Allowing Scripture to lead the prayer times has brought unity to the group, thus strengthening the time spent in prayer. When groups of four to six people continue the prayer time, everyone becomes involved. In these small groups one hears the hearts of others and can join with them in praying for common concerns.

A central focus for corporate prayer is important. For example, the Concert of Prayer's focus is to pray for revival and spiritual reawakening. Its goals are "prayer for God to reveal to the church the fullness of Christ as Lord in her midst (revival, renewal, awakening) and prayer for the resulting fulfillment of God's global cause through the church, among all the nations, including our own (missions, world evangelization, advancement of the Kingdom)."[1]

The corporate body finds its strength as it focuses on a specific purpose for prayer. It could be local, such as seeking God for an immediate decision for the church. It could be community-wide social concerns such as violence. Or it could be as big as praying for peace in the world. The specifics depend on the group of people.

This kind of corporate prayer is not something included briefly within a worship service but is a special time set apart for the purpose of seeking God's face together over a period of at least one to two hours. It may involve only one congregation, be a united meeting of churches within the community, or be clusters of churches from one denomination.

Use the following format as a guide for your own corporate prayer event. A sample prayer service is found on page 138. Invite people well in advance to prepare for this corporate time of praying. Make your gathered time celebrative. Include in your prayer time opportunities for praise, repentance, courage, visioning, unison prayer, prayer of commitment, and blessing.

Praise

Celebrate God together by singing praises and opening your hearts to experience God's presence. Often choruses such as "Majesty, Worship His Majesty" or "O Lord, Our Lord, How Majestic Is Thy Name in all the Earth" will express praise beautifully when sung as a body. This will help draw people to that place of unity for which Christ prayed so clearly in John 17.

Repentance

Sin will prevent God from hearing your prayers. Therefore, plan a way to help people to humble themselves and allow God to search their hearts as individuals. Singing a chorus such as "Search Me, O God" can lead into a time of silence allowing individuals to commune with God and make confessions as appropriate. Then break into groups of four to six people and confess any corporate sins that emerge. Isaiah 59:2 may be used: "But your iniquities have separated you from your God; your sins have hidden his face from you, so that he will not hear." Remember the promise in 1 John 1:9: "If we confess our sins, he is faithful and just and will forgive us our sins and purify us from all unrighteousness." To go beyond the general phrase of asking God to forgive your sins, be specific and name those sins as they are revealed. These may include apathy, indifference, or unbelief. Specifically naming the corporate sins moves the group in healthy ways. Your hearts are then ready for a more meaningful experience in prayer.

Courage

The changes that come as the result of your praying may be met with resistance.

Recognize where that resistance is coming from. It is usually a tool of the evil one to keep you from accomplishing what God is leading you to do. In groups of four to six people, anticipate what may be trying to prevent the church from moving forward and pray that God will give you courage and wisdom to address those in constructive ways. Something as simple as some one saying, "It's never been done that way before," can block people from taking steps of faith.

Envisioning

Ask God to help you envision what it is that you are being called to do. In groups of three or four, share what it would look like if that calling were to become reality. How would it be different from what is being experienced? Then pray that these things will come to pass. Scripture can be used to lift one's vision to God's promises and callings. Appropriate hymns or choruses can bring the small group prayer times to an end as you move to the next phase.

Praying Together

Invite the group to pray together, giving people the opportunity to voice their prayers for the church. This can be a spontaneous time for praying, or some people could be asked in advance to pray for some aspect of the prayer time or it can be a combination of the two. This allows everyone to hear the hearts of others.

Commitment

Once you have prayed in this manner and have heard God give guidance for next steps, pray for commitment. Someone may be asked in advance to voice this prayer. It is also a time for the group to make a commitment. Singing a hymn such as "O Jesus, I Have Promised" or a chorus such as "I Will Serve Thee" provides a corporate way to pray their commitment to carry out any direction given during the prayer time.

Blessing

Close the time with a blessing for the people and send them out equipped to fulfill their calling.

Some people fear the style of prayer just discussed because they think it takes away their opportunity to be free to the Spirit's movement in their own hearts. This style of praying unites people in their prayer focus and strengthens the power of prayer. The Spirit can speak to the group. In our personal prayer times, the Spirit can move into our own lives, but in corporate prayer we are blessed by being united in what the Spirit is saying to the group.

Opening your hearts to use a different format to pray together can be uplifting and inspiring. Trust God to make it an important and special time, the beginning of something powerful within the faith community.

SUMMARY

Setting aside extended times for prayer can be uplifting and precious. Corporate praying needs to involve everyone. With the use of hymns and choruses, guided with words of Scripture, prayer can be offered in groups of twos, threes, and fours. A pattern for such a prayer event would include times for praise, confession, courage, visioning, commitment, and blessing.

REFLECT AND RESPOND

Do you feel a yearning in your heart to see God move in more known ways as a faith community? Is there some specific concern or need that could draw you to gather for concerted prayer together? Study the Sample Prayer Service found on pages 138-150 and allow God to help you see how such an event could be held in your church, community, or denomination.

---

1 David Bryant, *Operation: Prayer II* (Wheaton, IL: Concerts of Prayer International, 1990), p. 6.

CHAPTER 13

Praying in the Community

Though Jesus respected the Sabbath worship, much of his time was spent in the community among poor and needy. The church leaders of that time, the Pharisees, criticized him. A woman, who was known in the community as a sinner, brought an alabaster jar of perfume and stood behind Jesus weeping. She began to wash his feet with her tears and dry them with her hair. The Pharisee said, "If this man were a prophet, he would know who is touching him and what kind of woman she is—that she is a sinner" (Luke 7:39). Jesus knew what was in the Pharisee's heart. He used the opportunity to teach him that this woman's sins, though many, were forgiven (Luke 7:36-50). Because Jesus mingled with sinners, he touched the lives of many people.

Many of our churches today are isolated from the communities in which they find themselves. This may happen for a variety of reasons. One problem is that the gap between those involved with the church and those not involved with the church is growing so wide that it becomes difficult to know how to communicate. Churches say they want more people to come to church or that they want to carry on a ministry but they are clueless as to what that ministry might be. Often that is because they are unfamiliar with the needs of their community.

In East Los Angeles, one church served as a government distribution center for cheese and honey. People who benefited from the cheese and honey were asked to fill out a form, including their name and address and a complete list of all those who lived in their house. The pastor, a Puerto Rican student, realized that list of names should be significant. Why were they allowed access to those people within their community? The church had never felt comfortable going door to door to invite people to church. At the suggestion of his professor, this pastor invited his church people to come an hour before their midweek prayer service. They would randomly take names from the list and, going in teams of three, visit a few of these families. They were to let the families know that there would be a prayer service later that evening in their church where they would pray for needs in the community. They asked if there were some needs for which this family would like prayer. To make sure there were no mix-ups, they asked the family to write their requests on a clipboard. They assured the family that they would be back next week to see how things were going. Though they never suggested that the family come to the church, within six months, the church had grown so much that they had to look for a new facility where they could meet.[1] What a wonderful way to become known in the community—a church that prays for needs in the neighborhood! God can show us creative ways to share his love with people in our communities.

COME PRAY

At one time, the church I was attending made an intentional effort to connect with people living within about a four-block radius. The church was well established. It was surrounded by beautiful old homes that were now being turned into apartment houses. Few of the church members lived in that vicinity. Through the evangelism task group, the church decided to host a hog roast on their large, shaded lawn. Brochures about the church were printed and fliers were made for those who were willing to walk door to door to invite people to the hog roast. At each home, we introduced ourselves and said that we were from the large church on the corner. We invited them to the hog roast and left the brochure and flier with them. The amazing thing was that we learned a lot about how people perceived us. Many said that they didn't think anyone could attend our church unless they were members. Others who were actively involved in their own churches were pleased to know that we were making the visits and reaching out into the neighborhood. At some places, the visitors were welcomed into the home for a longer visit.

People are much more open to hearing about God and praying than we give them credit. Approximately 225 people showed up for the hog roast while around seventy-five of us mingled to get acquainted with the people and learn some of their stories. One woman, for example, had been diagnosed with brain cancer. She had had surgery but had been told there was little else medically that could be done for her. Someone had visited her and had prayed for her healing. The woman was doing very well and was looking for a church home.

PRAYER WALKING.

In recent years a common way of praying for the community is to walk the streets and pray for those who live in the homes being passed. This is not a new concept. As far back as 180 A.D. there have been references to praying while walking. Hermas in *The Shepherd* wrote: "While then I am walking alone, I entreat the Lord that he will accomplish the revelations and visions which he showed me through his holy Church, that he may strengthen me and may give repentance to his servants which have stumbled, that his great and glorious name may be glorified.[2] It is also known that Saint Patrick, John Wycliffe, and George Fox did serious walks while praying.

Prayer walking, as it is known today, is an inexpensive, labor- effective means of corporate praying in the community. It has been defined as "praying on site with insight." Steve Hawthorne further explains that prayer walking "is intercessory prayer, praying in the very place in which you expect your prayers to be answered."[3]

Perhaps Joshua was the first to be introduced to the concept of prayer walking. When God was preparing him to become the leader for the Israelite people after Moses' death, the Lord told Joshua, "I will give you every place where you set your foot, as I promised Moses" (Joshua 1:3).

In recent years, many people and church groups have discovered the power of prayer while praying in the community. An Anglican church in England began prayer walking the ninety streets within the border of its parish. People committed to praying regularly for certain streets. After doing this for four years, the pastor said that prayer walking had become a common characteristic of their community. Even the local press had featured this in their paper. Had it made any difference in their community? The following was observed: "The crime rate has dropped, the spiritual atmosphere improved and slum housing has been replaced. Relationships have improved between ministers and local churches. And more people are joining the church."[4]

To agree to prayer walk is an important way to pray corporately for the neighborhood. The church will find it an experience in growth as they become more aware of the community. Just agreeing to walk regularly with a group of people gives strength to the effort.

Here are some ideas to get started. As a Sunday school class or a small Bible study group, pray together to seek God's will for committing to this plan. Determine where the prayer walk will be done and divide into teams of two or three people. Each week (or whatever schedule you plan) before going out, pray for God's protection of you and of your families, for sensitivity to the people within the community, and for God's guidance as you enter this adventure. As you walk along the streets, pray for each resident in the house or business. Pray that they recognize God's presence; that they will be responsive to those who bring the Gospel; that Satan will be bound in his attempts to blind them from receiving the Gospel and that they will accept Christ into their hearts. By the time you have quietly prayed for the people in one house, you will have moved on to the next house. Don't try to attract attention to yourself, but if someone wants to talk with you, be honest about what you are doing. The walk can take as long as you choose to do it, but forty-five to sixty minutes is a good way to begin.

Some of my friends discovered that there were people in the area who appeared to be hungry. They bought groceries for a family of four for one week. When they went prayer walking, they asked God to show them who should receive that food. This opened opportunities for praying in the community.

On one occasion, it had not been clear to whom the food should be given so they decided to ask a woman sitting on her front lawn if she knew anyone in the neighborhood who needed some food. After explaining what was behind the question, the woman timidly admitted that in fact she would fit that category. She and her husband had divorced, leaving her with small children. Her parents, who had been her support system, had moved away just weeks before. She said that her money had come to an end before the month was up and she was in need of food. What a joy it was to take the food. While placing it in her house, my friends explained to her that this was a practical way to show God's love. They wanted to pray with her. Did she have any special concerns for which they could pray?

On another occasion, it was decided that a large family, who occupied two large houses, would receive the food. When we delivered the food and told them we would like to pray with them before we left, they named a few things they were concerned about but then they asked if we remembered the nineteen-year-old girl who had been murdered on July 4 that year. We did remember. They said that the brother of the man who was charged with the murder lived two houses down from them. He was having a hard time with the whole situation. Would we pray for him? We would never have known about that community pain had we not been in the neighborhood.

MAKE YOUR HOME A POWER HOUSE.
There are other ways to be intentional in praying outside of your church. Make Your Home a Power House is the name given to one suggestion.[5] A group of people within the church commit to identify five neighbors, work associates, or unsaved persons whom the Lord lays on their hearts. They commit that they will pray five minutes a day, five days a week for five weeks. They will ask God to bless these people physically and provide health, protection, energy, and physical needs of food and clothing. They pray that they will enjoy adequate income and that they will have job satisfaction and a good work environment. They pray for inner peace, joy, and wisdom. They pray for healthy relationships with spouses, parents, children, friends, and if reconciliation needs to take place that will happen. They also pray for the spiritual health of these people. As the weeks go along, they ask God to show them how they can do small acts of kindness such as shoveling snow for their neighbor. And they pray that God will prepare the time when they can have a conversation about God's love with each of these people. Each week they plan to gather to hear what is happening in the lives of the many people for whom they are praying.

One couple shared that they had been praying for their neighbor, but they didn't seem to be making any headway. They asked if the whole group would join them in praying. That afternoon, the man who had been praying went outside to work on the lawn. He saw his neighbor get in his car and back out of the driveway, then drive back in the driveway. He got out of the car and walked into the yard where the man was working and simply said, "My wife and I have been thinking about going to church. I notice you go to church. Could we go with you?"[6] Some people would say this was just a coincidence, but certainly God had orchestrated this event.

Praying intentionally for people outside of the church not only has an impact on them but it impacts the pray-ers as well, for their faith in Jesus will increase as they see God working in the lives of those for whom they have prayed.

Summary

Jesus spent a lot of time mingling with people who were sinners. He demonstrated the need to pray for those who are not part of the church. Praying in the community makes one become aware of needs. Often it is through those needs that important ministries can begin.

Prayer walking is an old concept of praying on site with insight, praying where you expect your prayers to be answered. It is an intentional effort on the part of the church to pray for every home in designated areas over a period of time.

Making Your Home a Power House is another corporate way of praying for people. Those who commit to do this identify neighbors, work associates, or unsaved persons God brings to their attention. They pray for them five minutes a day for five days a week for five weeks. They trust God to help them see an act of kindness they can do to make contact with the person and pray for the opportunity to talk about God's love with the people. By doing it corporately they can encourage one another each week.

Though it is possible to pray by yourself as you walk or care about your neighbor, there is strength in doing it as a body of Christ. The commitment to each other will help you keep faithful, and as you share what God is doing your spiritual life will grow.

REFLECT AND RESPOND

Does it concern you that there are people in your community who may have never been introduced to Jesus? What is your attitude about praying on site with insight? Is God showing you something you could do to touch the lives of people through prayer in your community? Will you do it? How welcoming would your church be to newcomers from your neighborhood who might choose to worship with you?

---

1 Peter C. Wagner, *Churches That Pray* (Ventura, CA: Regal Books, 1993), pp. 178-179.
2 Graham Kendrick and John Houghton, *Prayerwalking* (Eastbourne, England: Kingsway Publications, 1990), p. 24.
3 Steve Hawthorne, "Prayerwalking" (*Body Life*, December, 1992), p. 1.
4 Wagner, Ibid., p. 178.
5 Alvin J. Vander Griend, *"Make Your Home a Power House"* (Grand Rapids, MI: HOPE Ministries, 1997), pp. 1-31.
6 Ibid, p. 20.
Other Resource
  Steve Hawthorne and Graham Kendrick, *Prayerwalking, Praying On Site With Insight* (Orlando, FL: Creation House, 1993).

CONCLUSION

My journey in prayer continues to be very important to me. I thank God for the teachings I have received along the way from my walk with him and from the many people who have encouraged me by sharing their experiences. I am grateful for opportunities to pass on those teachings as I lead seminars, write articles, and talk with others.

It is easy to hurry from one chapter to the next without pausing to experience the intimacy with God that has been shared through my stories and the stories of others. I hope you will take time to pause at the end of each chapter and reflect on its content.

Over the next month, experiment with some of the personal prayer styles included here or develop your intercessory skills. Let Scripture direct you as you pray for church leaders and other concerns. Try combining fasting with prayer and discover the clarity that comes when distractions are minimized to afford us the opportunity to focus on God.

No one is any more special to God than you. Your personal prayer life can mature and grow. The secret is to talk with God about big things and small things and then watch expectantly to see how God responds. The evidence may not be immediate or dramatic, but watch for the intermediate steps and acknowledge what God is about.

When your prayer life is strong, people will notice a difference in you. You will feel more confident. You will lead a more directed life. You will be more caring because, as you interact at a deeper level, you will take on more of the characteristics of your intimate Friend.

I long for the day when the church will once again take a more central place in our lives. You have been given some tools to help you find ways to pray together as a body of believers. Don't be discouraged if only a few join you to pray corporately at first. Even when a major prayer event is included in a conference, only 10 percent will choose to attend that session. Remember that even when two or three gather in Jesus' name, he promises to be present and God's power can be released. Expect to see God honor your efforts and find ways to share what God is doing as you meet faithfully to pray together. When it becomes important to you, in time, it will become important to others as they see results related to your praying.

Ask God to show you others who are interested in a vital walk with God. I pray that through a more intentional emphasis on prayer, your church will experience God in fresh and real ways. Your faith will grow and impact the lives of others in your community and throughout the world.

As you close this book, I trust that you will join those who are on an adventure in deepening prayer. Keep your heart in tune; listen for God to initiate a conversation with you. Don't hesitate to lift your praise and thanks to God and to share what you learn with others. May this book be a stepping-stone to a richer understanding of God for you and for your church.

ACTIVITY 1

Use Scripture to Inform Prayer

In Chapter 2, we suggested that you allow Scripture to form you as you pray. In other words, instead of studying the passage for information, look at it in the light of how it can form you and your reactions in your daily living. As you see yourself in the passage, there may be things that you and God need to talk together about. Take time to let God help you understand the passage and those places in your life where you may need to make some changes. Use these steps to help you:

1. Select a short passage of Scripture for meditation.
2. Read it through once in its entirety.
3. Go back slowly through the passage guided by questions such as these:
   - Do you see yourself in any of the people involved in this passage?
   - Had you been present, how would you have reacted?
   - What does God want you to see about yourself in the light of this passage?
   - Ask God to reveal more of himself to you through this passage.

4. Reflect on the insights you are given. Do you need to make a confession? Is there an assignment to be carried out? Do you need to adjust your attitude?
5. Let your insights, reactions, and responses to this passage open up fresh avenues for conversation with God.

For example, use the story of blind Bartimaeus in Mark 10:46-52 and follow these steps. Read it through. Put the story into your own words to help open the passage up.

Somehow Bartimaeus learned that Jesus was leaving Jericho and would be passing on a certain road. He probably had heard about Jesus and was determined to be among the crowd that was gathering to see Jesus. Maybe he had arranged for someone to get him there early. Bartimaeus couldn't see when Jesus came within view but he heard people in the crowd passing the word along, announcing that Jesus had been sighted. Bartimaeus shouted out, "Jesus, Son of David, have mercy on me!" (v. 47). The crowd was embarrassed by that outburst and sternly ordered him to be quiet. Probably those near him put their hands on his shoulder to try to get him to sit back down and be still. Bartimaeus was not going to let this opportunity pass him by. He shouted again, "Son of David, have mercy on me!" (v. 48). The crowd was astounded. Jesus came near the place where the blind man was and stopped. He said, "Call him." (v.49). The man sprang up and threw off his cloak, the symbol of a beggar, and found his way to Jesus. The crowd had to swallow their pride. Maybe they helped him find his way to Jesus. What would happen when Jesus and the man met? Were they about to witness a healing miracle? Jesus' question to the blind man was, "What do you want me to do for you?" (v. 51). Wouldn't you think that Jesus would know what a blind man wanted? Bartimaeus, without hesitation, said, "Rabbi, I want to see" (v. 51). Jesus responded by telling him that his faith had made him well. He regained his sight and followed Jesus on the way.

Slowly go back over the passage, reflecting on questions such as those suggested. Do you see yourself as a member of the crowd, putting down those less fortunate, thinking yourself to be better than they? Or are you the blind man? Do you have some need that you want to ask Jesus about? What is it that you throw off when you are talking with Jesus? The blind man must have known that he would no longer need that cloak, so strong was his faith that Jesus would give him sight. Do you continue to hang on to your burden so tightly that Jesus doesn't have a chance to take the load from you? Are you clear about what it is you want Jesus to do for you? Does Jesus see your faith? How do you think you would have reacted if you had been present at this place? What new insight is God giving you about yourself? About God? Is God asking you to make a change in your life? Is God giving you an assignment?

In the silence of your heart, listen to what God may have to say to you. Enter into a conversation with God that will bring clarity and direction for your life. When you return to your daily task, be sensitive to your behavior and responses. Are they consistent with the new understanding you have gained? Are you letting the Scripture form you?

If this has been a helpful way to grow in your praying, find other passages and use the same pattern. Suggestions might be Matthew 8:1-4 and Luke 18:9-14.

ACTIVITY 2

Pray with a Parable

People hear at the level they understand. When Jesus used parables, sometimes people heard only the earthly story. Other times, they saw a truth that Jesus was trying to help them see. Joyce Huggett, in her book *Praying the Parables*, tells us how the parables can lead us into a deeper prayer life.

First, read the parable at the level of the earthly story. Then slowly look for the deeper truths through the light of the Holy Spirit. Consider how those truths can be lived out in your life. Bring those matters to God in prayer and expect God to give you insights and understanding.

Use the familiar parable of the Good Samaritan. Read it from Luke 10:25-37. Then try to imagine how the original audience would have heard that story.

Jesus was no doubt talking with a group of Pharisees and teachers of the law. A religious expert stepped forward. By Middle Eastern custom, he politely addressed Jesus as Teacher, but there was something about his body language that made those gathered around know that his motive was quite the opposite. In fact, the passage says that he "stood up to test Jesus" (v. 25).

Imagine yourself as an audience to this conversation. You hear it from the perspective of the Pharisees and teachers of the law. The young man has achieved a lot in his short life and probably thought it would be a good idea to get this "eternal life" he'd been hearing about through Jesus. He asked Jesus, "What must I do to inherit eternal life?" (v. 25).

Jesus respected the young man and challenged him from the perspective of his knowledge. He said, "What is written in the law? How do you read it?" (v. 26). The young expert let the words flow eloquently from his lips: "Love the Lord your God with all your heart, and with all your soul, and with all your strength, and with all your mind; and your neighbor as yourself" (v. 27).

Jesus' response was simple, "You have answered correctly. Do this and you will live" (v. 28). The religious expert, often referred to as a lawyer, was not content with that answer. He wanted Jesus to explain who his neighbor was.

Jesus then told the parable known as The Good Samaritan. Listen to this story as if you were a Pharisee. When Jesus started to talk about a man going down from Jerusalem to Jericho, see in your mind seventeen miles of hot and hostile desert, dangerous and lonely territory. You think it unwise for a person, like yourself, to travel that road alone. As Jesus continued the story, sure enough the man "fell into the hands of robbers. They stripped him of his clothes, beat him and went away, leaving him half dead" (v. 30).

"A priest happened to be going down the same road, and when he saw the man, he passed by on the other side" (v. 31). Reading that sentence in our present context causes grief that a recognized man of God would pass by. How could he be so cold hearted? But for those who first heard this story, the priest had responded appropriately. After all, he was expected to give to a good man, not to a sinner. How could he know at that stage whether he was a good man? On one hand, being in such an unsafe area made him nervous because he knew that he could face the same tragedy. On the other hand, if he remained to offer help and others saw him, they would probably accuse him of the crime. It is possible he was on a mission for which stopping to help a person like this would render him unclean to perform his duty. The words from Leviticus (19:17-18), which essentially says that your neighbor is someone of your own kind, could have also been the basis for his behavior. When a person was unable to speak and was stripped of his clothing, how could the priest know if he was his 'neighbor'? So from the Pharisees' perspective, this priest did the right thing.

"So, too, a Levite, when he came to the place and saw him, passed by on the other side" (v. 32). Levites were also religious people. They served as temple assistants and held responsibilities at a lower rank than the priest. He may have known that the priest passed this same person, and since he didn't stick around, the Levite felt no compunction to get involved either.

The Pharisees couldn't find fault with the behavior of these religious leaders. They were prepared for a third person to be a layman. But when Jesus said that this person was a Samaritan, they were befuddled. After all, the Jews hated the Samaritans. They were considered half-breeds. They remembered the recent incident where the Samaritans defiled the Temple during the Passover. Tension was mounting.

Jesus then said, "When he saw him, he took pity on him. He went to him and bandaged his wounds, pouring on oil and wine" (v. 33-34). This Samaritan man responded from a gut level compassion. He came to the place. He saw the injured man. He cared about him and acted with compassion. He got off his donkey to pour in the oil and wine and bandaged the man's wounds. He acted as a servant as he put the man on his donkey and took him to an inn.

The Pharisees would know that there would be no inn nearby. The good Samaritan would have to interrupt his journey and go either to Jerusalem or Jericho to find an inn. Both of those cities would be dangerous for him since both cities were Jewish places. They also knew that for this man to provide this kind of care, he was taking a huge risk. People could easily accuse him of the crime. Why would he choose to take such a risk?

In that same context, the Samaritan man knew that if he took the man to the inn and left him at the door, one of two things could easily happen. 1) He could be beaten again by others. 2) The innkeeper could sell him as a slave. The only compassionate alternative would be for him to ask for care for the man and assure payment on his behalf. The story indicates that he chose to do the latter.

At the conclusion of the story, Jesus turned to the young man who had asked the question and simply said, "Which of these three do you think was a neighbor to the man who fell into the hands of robbers?" (v. 36). What could the young man say? It was so obvious that the neighbor was the one who showed mercy. Jesus told him "Go and do likewise" (v. 37).

Parables are earthly stories with heavenly meanings. No doubt Jesus was addressing the lawyer's questions on two levels. Jesus was suggesting that if the young man seriously wanted to know who his neighbor was so that he could love him as he loved himself, then he needed to see himself as the neighbor and reach out to anyone in need such as the Samaritan did. But on another level, Jesus was responding to a desire to understand justification and the way to inherit eternal life. The lawyer needed to see himself as the wounded man. He needed to know that God would come at great cost and bind up his wounds.

There is no record of how the young expert reacted to Jesus' parable. The question is how do you respond to this parable in your present context? Jesus raised several issues in this parable. There are questions of ethics, race, risk-taking, compassion, justice, and oppression. As you consider these issues, you might recall instances when you could have responded in a better way.

A friend of mine lived about a block away from a family she knew was having extreme marital problems. As she drove by one afternoon, she saw the mother out with her children. She felt God's nudges that she should stop and offer to take care of the children so the mother could get some rest, but there were other things on her agenda and she drove on by thinking that another day she would get to it. Before she arranged to do that, the father in that family came one evening, shot and killed the mother, and then did the same to himself. My friend learned a very big lesson that day. When God speaks to you about something, God is speaking for now, not for another time when it may be more convenient.

A nurse tells how praying with this parable, God came to her so helpfully. She found herself in the sandals of the rescuer. She was exhausted and in pain, grieving for the refugees among whom she had been working and whom she had had to leave suddenly. She was advised to imagine that the body by the side of the road was one of the refugees she had been forced to leave behind. When she did that, something incredible happened to her. In her words, she described it thus: "I saw the body lying there and I went up to it. I thought it was one of the refugee women I knew. I was about to dress her wounds when, suddenly, I realized that the body wasn't the woman's after all. It was Jesus. I took him in my arms and dressed his wounds. I can't explain what that did to me."[1]

Praying with this parable allows you to wrestle with the many issues Jesus raised. Find a quiet place where you can be uninterrupted. Use the following questions as a guide to pray with this parable. Ask God to reveal new insights to you and to show you how to deepen your understanding of God. Be open to hear God speak to you as you pray.

1. Which of the characters in the story do you identify with?

   the man who fell among the robbers
   the Good Samaritan
   the priest
   the innkeeper
   the Levite

   Imagine the scene with this character as if it were a news cast without commentary. How would you relate to this incident?

2. What opportunities for serving others have come across your path this week? How did you respond? Did you turn your back on injustice or oppression when you were given the opportunity to speak or work for justice or peace? Why did you respond as you did? Take time to let God help you recall your behavior. Rejoice

if you have always been faithful but cautiously reflect on those times when you knew you should be helpful but you chose to put it off and then it was too late.
3. Do you feel drained from giving and giving? In the silence of your heart, ask Jesus to come and refill you with God's Spirit so your response to God's nudging will be more timely.
4. Have you felt wounded or abandoned and longed for a "neighbor" to help you? Who came to you when you were in need? What happened to you? How did it feel? Talk with God about that.
5. Jesus carefully included in this story a racial clash. Ask God to help you look at yourself as you encounter people of other cultures or faith traditions. Do you harbor resentments or grudges toward persons of a different color or different perspectives on life? How do you handle encounters with these people?
6. Jesus could see that the religious laws misled so many people. They thought they were pleasing God, when, in fact, they were bringing God anguish. Look at yourself or your church and ask God to show you how you may be bringing anguish to God. Take time to seek God's guidance on how to address the issues that you are made aware of.
7. Consider again who the Good Samaritan really was. When robbers took so much away from the wounded man, the Good Samaritan generously paid for the man's care. When the robbers wounded him and left him for dead, the Good Samaritan held him in his arms. The robbers turned their backs on the man while

the Good Samaritan promised not to forsake him. The Good Samaritan in this story represents God. As you pray with this parable, is there some place in your life you need Jesus to come and minister to you?

Quietly let God open your mind to other issues that this story may touch in your life. Patiently allow God to let you look into your life and fill you with the desire to be more responsive to God's ways and purposes.

SUMMARY

Using the parables to guide your prayer time will often raise important questions that God wants to discuss with you. Look beyond the story to the deeper truths Jesus is addressing. In the parable of the Good Samaritan, Jesus raises questions about ethics, about race, about risk taking, about compassion, and about God's intervention when people are treated unjustly or oppressed. Realize that Jesus is not saying to go and bandage the wounds of everyone everywhere, but to receive the divine love so that when the call comes, you are ready to respond and let Christ's love flow through you.

REFLECT AND RESPOND

Look at other parables with the keen desire to let Jesus teach you deeper truths, and then enter your prayer time responding to those truths in your own life.

---

1 Joyce Huggett, *Praying the Parables* (Downers Grove, IL: InterVarsity Press, 1996), p. 105.

ACTIVITY 3

Plan for a Corporate Prayer Event

God wants to demonstrate his love and power among us and within the church in more ways than we realize. Planning a Prayer Event can be a powerful way of acknowledging God's love and power and gaining direction for things that we face. For this to be an effective and important event there needs to be adequate preparation.

PREPARATION

The designated planning group needs prayerfully and boldly to seek God's leading in planning and preparing for such an event. Be specific why you are calling people to pray. Will it be for a decision to be made within the church? Will it be for revival and renewal? Will it be broader than one faith community?

Consider who will be invited to attend. Will it be for your church only? Will you invite the churches of your community? In the event, you are focusing on something affecting your denomination, should you invite nearby churches of your own faith to join you?

Where will you be gathering? That should be determined by the size of the group you invite. A community-wide event

PLAN FOR A CORPORATE PRAYER EVENT

may need to be held in a community building large enough to accommodate the group. In that case, you would probably want to involve people from the different churches to make the plans for such an event.

Publicize the event as far and wide as you can. Do it with enthusiasm and anticipation. Announce it well in advance so people can plan to include it on their busy calendars.

Under-gird the whole event with prayer. Pastors may want to set aside times for prayer together. Include this event in prayers during worship. If there are small groups, invite them to make this event a matter of prayer. God likes to know that this is seen as something very important in the life of the congregation.

Arrange for song leaders and let them know how important the music will be. Plan for one leadership person who is sensitive to the Spirit's leading to move the group together. Invite some people to come prepared to pray at specific times during the session. Involve others in ushering responsibilities and arranging for the location.

Sample prayer service focused on becoming a house of Prayer

Introduction

Leader: Welcome to each of you. We have the delightful opportunity to pray together and experience corporately what God is saying to our church. Your presence encourages us that you share in the desire to see our church become the house of prayer that Jesus described when he said, "My house will be called a house of prayer" (Matthew 21:13). Expect God to be very present with us, to reveal new insights and to equip us to have a more intimate relationship with him. Let's open our hearts to God by singing songs inviting us to worship and praise.

Song Leader: *(Lead the group in some hymns or choruses that call people to focus on God. Some suggestions are "How Great Thou Art," "Majesty, Worship His Majesty," "Bless the Lord," "To God Be the Glory," "Let's Just Praise the Lord," "Holy, Holy, Holy," "His Name Is Wonderful." The length of time for this will be determined by the length of time you anticipate for the service. If it is two hours, you could devote as much as fifteen minutes but make it a worshipful time. This will set the tone for the whole event.)*

Leader: Today we have gathered for the purpose of seeking God's leading for helping our church to become a powerhouse of prayer. This may be a different format than you have experienced before. Enter this time with expectation. Be open to a different way of talking with God together. Relax in the presence of God. Let songs and Scripture help us focus our thoughts. You will be guided through singing, praying together, sometimes in pairs, sometimes in small groups, and sometimes as a whole. There will be times for silent prayer. We trust you will open your hearts to what God has to teach us today and that you will anticipate direction and be willing to commit yourselves to move our church into becoming a power house of prayer.

Perhaps you hurried to come today and are still dealing with things that might distract you from giving your full attention to prayer. We will take a couple of minutes for you to divide into pairs. Introduce yourself to the other if you don't know them. Then share with the other person one thing that could keep you from focusing your attention on the purpose for being here. Make it brief so each of you can share. Then pray for each other that God will care for that concern and allow you to be completely attentive.

Response: *(Allow no more than three minutes for this. There will be audible humming as people pray for one another. The leader should remain in place quietly praying.)*

Song Leader: *(Begin singing a chorus or one verse of a hymn to close this time together. Suggested songs might be "Where the Spirit of the Lord is" or "Fill My Cup, Lord.")*

ACKNOWLEDGE GOD'S PRESENCE

Leader: Let us acknowledge God's invitation to pray as we begin a time of prayer. Enter into this time in an attitude of prayer whether that is with your eyes closed, kneeling, or focusing on some object. God is present in this place as we go to prayer. Listen to Jesus' words: "For where two or three come together in my name, there am I with them" (Matthew 18:20). God invites us to "Call upon me and come and pray to me, and I will listen to you" (Jeremiah 29:12). The Psalmist says, "The Lord is near to all who call on him, to all who call on him in truth" (Psalm 145:18).

COME PRAY

(Pause between each passage to allow time for the words to sink into the hearts of people gathered. Don't feel hurried. Let the Spirit move among the group.)

Focus your thoughts on Jesus as you move into this time of prayer. Imagine Jesus sitting in the chair beside you. You can see the love in his eyes and when you shake his hand, you feel the scars put there on behalf of all of us gathered. *(Give time for silence.)*

Response: *(Silence as people focus on Jesus.)*

Leader: *(Close this silence with a prayer acknowledging God's presence in this place or use this suggested prayer.)* God, we have gathered to honor and praise you. Thank you for each person who is here. Thank you for taking our cares and burdens so all can focus on you. Guide us as we look to you to help us understand what becoming a house of prayer means for this church and help us to obey. Make us willing to change some things so that we can release your power among us. Give us discernment to see what really matters to you and free us from the petty things that the evil one uses to distract us. We look to you as we continue in our time of prayer together. Amen.

Praise/Rejoice

Leader *(continues)***:** Part of praying is giving God praise and acknowledging God's faithfulness. We have a lot of things for which we can give praise. The next few moments will be given to praising God. Divide into groups of four. Introduce yourselves to each other. Then go around the group, turning to the person on your right and then on your left and thank God for that person. If you know the person you may want to add a special thanks for something you particularly appreciate about that person.

Response: *(Divide into groups of four and give thanks for each other.)*

Song Leader: *(Allow time for this experience, gauging it as you notice groups getting finished with this exercise. Close by singing a chorus or hymn. A suggestion would be "O How He Loves You and Me." People may need a little time to conclude, so don't be surprised if people continue praying as you start singing. Repeat the chorus if needed until people are done.)*

Leader: God is calling people to pray in unprecedented ways. Before Jesus ascended to heaven, the disciples were lost, their leader was gone and they weren't sure of the direction they should take. Jesus told them to stay in Jerusalem and wait for the promise of the Father (Acts 1:4). What did waiting mean? The disciples went to the upper room and constantly devoted themselves to prayer (Acts 1:14). They were filled with the Holy Spirit and were empowered to carry the message of Christ all over the world just as Jesus had promised (Acts 1:8). Their power came as they prayed. God wants to do something new among us. Interest in prayer has been piqued around the world, and historically, when that happens, there has been a spiritual awakening. God is also doing some wonderful things around us in answer to the prayers of many.

(At this point talk about some of the things you are aware of that God is doing in your midst, in your community, and/ or the world. Has someone been healed? Has God provided for some urgent need for the church or in your life? Share something from your own experience.) Do you have a praise that you would like to share? *(For the next few moments, give thanks and praise to God. Keep it brief. It may only be one sentence. When a person has finished sharing, say:)* Let's repeat together, "We give you our praise, O Lord." Where is God at work in your life or the life of your church?

(Invite people from the group to give praise for what God is doing in their lives or church. If you want to, use a blackboard or newsprint to list the things God is doing around you.)

Response: *(Give time for the group to share their stories of praise and lead them to repeat:* "We give you our praise, O Lord" *after each person has shared. Don't hurry this time but let it be an important part of praying.)*

Leader: *(When it seems appropriate, close this time with a prayer of praise. Feel a freedom to lift your hands in praise during this section.)* "Thank you, God for accepting these prayers of praise." *(Then share from Hebrews 13:15.)* "...let us continually offer to God a sacrifice of praise—the fruit of lips that confess his name."

Repent/Confess

Leader *(continues):* We move to confession. We have within us a desire to become a house of prayer. We are aware that the prayer life of this church could be stronger.

Yet there may be things that are barriers to this happening. Nehemiah faced a time when he got the news about his people back in Jerusalem who were in great trouble. We are told that he went to God in prayer and simply said, "I confess the sins we Israelites, including myself and my father's house, have committed against you" (Nehemiah 1:6). Then he proceeded to name some of them: "We have acted very wickedly toward you. We have not obeyed the commands, decrees and laws you gave your servant Moses" (Nehemiah 1:7). Nehemiah knew that the place to begin was to make sure that his heart was right with God. He prayed not only for himself but for the people. Isaiah 59:2 says "But your iniquities have separated you from you God; your sins have hidden his face from you so that he will not hear." Naming the sins as he knew them were very important in the process of knowing the next steps. In silence, let God examine your heart as individuals. If there are sins that need to be confessed, do that quietly in the silence of your heart. 1 John 1:9 says "If we confess our sins, he is faithful and just and will forgive us our sins and purify us from all unrighteousness."

Response: *(Let people silently make their personal confessions.)*

Leader: *(Close this time simply by saying "Amen.")* Go back to your groups of four. This is a time for the four of you to ask God if there are things within your church that prevent you from becoming a powerful house of prayer. Is there apathy among you? Indifference? Lack of commitment? Unbelief? Lack of teaching?

Individualism? Whatever is revealed, confess each of them in prayer within your group.

Response: *(Allow time for people to enter seriously into letting God examine their hearts as a body of faith.)*

Leader: *(When it seems appropriate, offer a prayer thanking God for hearing the confessions of this body of believers and for forgiving the corporate sins.)*

COURAGE TO OVERCOME RESISTANCES

Leader *(continues):* The evil one becomes very angry when prayer becomes strong. As the church moves to a more intentional and effective prayer life, there will be obstacles that will come. Recognize them for what they are—attempts to thwart your efforts to become a house of prayer. Those obstacles may come in the form of people saying, "We've never done it this way before." There may be others who will try to discourage participation in your efforts. Some may say that prayer is a waste of time or that prayer doesn't work. Don't be overcome by the negatives but trust God to give you wisdom to overcome those resistances. If you grow discouraged, ask God to give you power over the discouragement.

Knowing that there will be opposition to the church becoming a house of prayer, anticipate what may try to prevent your church from developing a more vital corporate prayer life. In groups of four, discuss and try to identify what those obstacles may be. Then go to prayer and ask God to give you discernment to identify where these obstacles are coming from and to give you power and courage to overcome them. Expect God to empower you and to make a difference.

Song Leader: *(Close this section with a hymn or chorus. A suggestion might be "He Is Lord.")*

ENVISION YOUR CHURCH AS A POWER HOUSE OF PRAYER

Leader: Jesus said, "It is written, 'My house will be called a house of prayer'" (Matthew 21:13). What would it look like if your church became known as a house of prayer? In the early church, we get a glimpse of what the church looked like. Listen to these words in Acts 2:42. "They devoted themselves to the apostles' teaching and to the fellowship, to the breaking of bread and to prayer." And from Acts 2:47: "And the Lord added to their number daily those who were being saved." What we see is a church whose priorities included teaching, fellowship, breaking of bread, and PRAYER—and many were saved daily!

In the next few moments in your groups of four, discuss things that you think will happen if your church becomes a house of prayer. How would it be different?

Response: *(Allow the group to talk together, envision what their church could become.)*

Leader: *(After a few moments of sharing, call the group to pray as a whole body. Invite the group to stand together. Make a circle if that is appropriate.)* You have shared various things in your groups that would be different if this faith community were to become a house of prayer.

Now is our time to pray and ask God to help the church to become a house of prayer. Mention the things that you have envisioned and pray for wisdom and courage over the rough spots. Whatever God is laying on your heart just now, let us pray. This is our opportunity to talk and hear each other's hearts as we talk with God on behalf of the church.

(If you think it will be hard to get started, you may want to ask one or two people in advance to be prepared to pray at this point but let it be as spontaneous as possible. Don't be afraid of silence. Allow time for the timid ones to get courage to voice their prayers.)

Response: *(This can be a very exciting time as people share with the group and God what they envision God wants to do in making your church a house of prayer. You may want to be prepared to take notes for discussion at a later time.)*

COMMITMENT

Leader: Do you feel God's yearning to walk with you intimately both as individuals and as a church? Do you feel a fresh passion for being available to God even if it means passing through uncharted waters? The disciples in Acts 4 were faced with a lot of persecution yet instead of focusing on the persecution, they prayed, "Now, Lord, consider their threats and enable your servants to speak your word with great boldness. Stretch out your hand to heal and perform miraculous signs and wonders through the name of your holy servant Jesus" (Acts 4:29-30). Friends, that is commitment to Jesus.

Can you make that kind of commitment to Jesus and boldly speak out and take the steps to lead your church to become the House of Prayer through which many people will come into an intimate relationship with Christ?

(You can acknowledge that it is sometimes hard for people to make a commitment but that is what it will take. If you sense that people want to discuss making a commitment to see that the next steps are taken to bring the faith community to being a house of prayer, give that opportunity. Close this section by either you, or someone you have arranged to do so, giving a prayer of commitment. Acknowledge with gratitude God's presence with you as you have prayed for guidance and direction for the church to become a house of prayer. Thank God for guidance given. Offer the body gathered to God to be obedient in fulfilling God's plan for them to become a house of prayer. Pray that each person present will be open to doing his/her part to grow in prayer life and together in the life of the whole church. Trust God to give you the passion and vision to make a difference.)

Song Leader: *(Close with a chorus or hymn that fits the mood of the moment. A suggestion might be "In My Life, Lord, Be Glorified." Be sure to sing the second verse, which says "In my church, Lord, be glorified.")*

BLESSING

Leader: *(Speak with enthusiasm and celebration as you close this service.)* This has been a wonderful time of sharing and praying together. You may have thought two hours *(or however long it has been)* would be a long time to pray. Have you felt blessed by being here? Let's give thanks and praise to God by singing, in closing, "My Tribute" or Couch's "To God Be the Glory."

Song Leader: *(Ask the group to stand and lead them in singing the above hymn or one of your choice.)*

Leader: *(Close with a blessing such as follows.)* We celebrate God's power to fill us with the Holy Spirit. May the God of peace become a very intimate Friend of each of us as we grow in our relationship with God through prayer. May this community become more aware of the ministry of this church and see this faith community as a people who pray and whose prayers give evidence of God's hearing. May we all be given a desire to be bold in ministry and may we truly experience God's love and power. Go in the knowledge of God's presence in the life of each person here. Expect great things from God and attempt great things for God.

RESOURCES

BOOKS

Anderson, Leith. *When God Says No.* Minneapolis, Minn.: Bethany Press, 1996.

Blackaby, Henry. *Experiencing God.* Nashville: Lifeway Press, 1990.

Blackaby, Henry and Claude V. King. *Experiencing God.* Nashville: Broadman and Holman, 1994.

Bright, Bill. *The Coming Revival: America's Call to Fast, Pray, and 'Seek God's Face.'* Orlando, Fla.: NewLife Publications, 1995.

Bryant, David. *Operation: Prayer II.* Wheaton, Ill.: Concerts of Prayer International, 1990.

Cedar, Paul. *A Life of Prayer.* Nashville: Word Publishing, 1998.

Christenson, Evelyn. *What Happens When Women Pray.* Colorado Springs: Chariot Victor Publishing, 1975.

Cornwall, Judson. *Praying the Scriptures.* Lake Mary, Fla.: Creation House, 1988.

Eastman, Dick. *The Hour That Changes the World.* Grand Rapids, Mich.: Baker Book House, 1978.

Foster, Richard. *Celebration of Discipline*. San Francisco: Harper & Row, 1978.
Hawthorne, Steve and Graham Kendrick. *Prayerwalking: Praying on Site with Insight*. Orlando, Fla.: Creation House, 1993.
Holland, Grace and Fred. *Talking with God*. Kisumu, Kenya: Evangel Publishing House, 1972.
Huggett, Joyce. *Praying the Parables*. Downers Grove, Ill.: InterVarsity Press, 1996.
Hybels, Bill. *Too Busy Not to Pray*. Downers Grove, Ill.: InterVarsity Press, 1988.
Jacobs, Cindy. *Possessing the Gates of the Enemy*. Grand Rapids, Mich.: Chosen Books, 1991.
_____. *The Voice of God*. Ventura, Calif.: Regal Books, 1995.
Jeremiah, David. *Prayer: the Great Adventure*. Sisters, Ore.: Multnomah Publishers, Inc., 1997.
Kendrick, Graham and John Houghton. *Prayerwalking*. Eastbourne, England: Kingsway Publications, 1990.
Kierkegaard, Søren. *Christian Discourses*. Trans. Walter Lowie. Oxford: Oxford University Press, 1940.
Martin, Glen and Dian Ginter. *Power House*. Nashville: Broadman and Holman, 1994.
Maxwell, John. *Partners in Prayer*. Nashville, Tenn.: Thomas Nelson Publishers, 1996.
Mulholland, Robert M. Jr. *Shaped by the Word*. Nashville: The Upper Room, 1985.
Rinker, Roselind. *Learning Conversational Prayer*. Collegeville, Minn.: The Liturgical Press, 1992.

Sheets, Dutch. *Intercessory Prayer*. Ventura, Calif.: Regal Books, 1996.

Thomas, Anne and Mary Glenn Hadley. *Preparing Hearts and Minds*. Richmond, Ind.: Friends United Press, 1998.

Vander Griend, Alvin J. *Make Your Home a Power House*. Grand Rapids, Mich.: HOPE Ministries, 1997.

Wagner, Peter. *Churches That Pray*. Ventura, Calif.: Regal Books, 1993.

_____. *Prayer Shield*. Ventura, Calif.: Regal Books, 1992.

_____. *Warfare Prayer*. Ventura, Calif.: Regal Books, 1992.

www.ingramcontent.com/pod-product-compliance
Lightning Source LLC
Chambersburg PA
CBHW050639160426
43194CB00010B/1734